Presented To:

_____

From:

_____

Date:

_____

REVIVAL HUNGER

REVIVAL HUNGER

FINDING GENUINE REVIVAL AMONG FLUFF AND HYPE

JAMES LEVESQUE

DESTINY IMAGE® PUBLISHERS, INC.

P.O. Box 310, Shippensburg, PA 17257-0310

"Promoting Inspired Lives."

This book and all other Destiny Image, Revival Press, MercyPlace, Fresh Bread, Destiny Image Fiction, and Treasure House books are available at Christian bookstores and distributors worldwide.

For a U.S. bookstore nearest you, call **1-800-722-6774.**

For more information on foreign distributors, call **717-532-3040.**

Reach us on the Internet: **www.destinyimage.com.**

ISBN 13 TP: 978-0-7684-3942-7

ISBN 13 Ebook: 978-0-7684-8943-9

For Worldwide Distribution, Printed in the U.S.A.

1 2 3 4 5 6 7 8 / 15 14 13 12 11

DEDICATION

I would like to dedicate this book to my wife, Debbie. You encourage me every step of the way to fulfill the call God has for us, and I am so thankful that we can live this amazing dream together. We are just getting started, "Lovie."

ENDORSEMENTS

James Levesque brings a challenge to the Body of Christ to surrender all so that the fullness of God's glory may be revealed. Let desperation for revival and transformation be cultivated in your heart as you read the pages of this book.

Ché Ahn
Senior Pastor, HROCK Church,
Pasadena, California
President, Harvest International Ministry
International Chancellor, Wagner Leadership Institute

James Levesque has written more than a story. It is a manual for overcomers. He is an example to all who know him of one who has refused to live in the status quo. This book will stretch you, reshape you, and give you thoughts to chew on for days to come. Read it as a hungry person would sit down to a feast, for this book is a spiritual feast! James has given us a treasure, so scoop it up and put it into your life. You'll be glad you did!"

Brian Simmons
Stairway Ministries
President, Apostolic Resource Center

James is not a theologian, yet when you read this book, you will confront profound theological truths about the life of the Spirit. By reading this book you will see how the Holy Spirit inscribed the life of Jesus in the heart of a willing soul. Through the simple willingness to believe and the unwillingness to pretend, you can discover the life of Jesus being lived out through you as well.

Pastor Mark Spitsbergen
Abiding Place Ministries,
San Diego, California

The works of Jesus and the heart of God are being given a powerful voice through lives of radical faith, simple obedience, and a heart to hear what God is saying in this hour. These are those who are beginning to emerge in great power as true ambassadors of God in these coming days. In his book *Revival Hunger*, James Levesque shares from personal testimonies, scriptural insight, and prophetic encounters keys to living a life devoted to knowing God and making Him known. It is sure to fan the embers of your faith as it stirs and provokes you to believe for more. This is more than a book; it is a challenge to a generation to "Give it all to Jesus!"

Jason Hooper
Revivalist, Jason Hooper Ministries
www.jasonhooper.org

The book you hold in your hands is not a message James preaches; it is the message he lives. The first time I heard James speak was also the first time I experienced not knowing whether I was in my body or out of it. I am forever changed by what happened to me that weekend. I am forever changed by the things you are about to read. This book challenges you to shed religion and truly encounter God.

Seth Dahl
Children's Pastor, Bethel Church,
Redding, California

With youthful passion and zeal, James encourages us to "get real," to "touch God," and to bring in the Harvest with power and love. I was greatly encouraged as this young leader, true to the high standard of the Kingdom, shows us all how to take the high ground.

John Arnott
President, Catch the Fire Ministries

Throughout our years of ministry, the Lord has allowed me, on occasion, to recognize incredible gifting and destiny on select individuals. The Bible tells us that the Lord puts His incredible treasures in earthen vessels. This oftentimes requires that we recognize people according to the Spirit, not according to historical background, appearance or educational status. That was the case when I first met James Levesque. In our first encounter, the Lord clearly identified this young man as a great last-day champion of the Kingdom set apart for the Lord. The Holy Spirit even allowed us a small part in releasing a commissioning on his life.

The book that you hold in your hand is a portion of that fruit. It has been a great joy to watch the Lord develop James' character, integrity, and spiritual attributes. He has an incredible hunger for the harvest and the presentation of the Gospel through demonstration of the Spirit. There is something uniquely woven into the spiritual DNA of these young champions that will not allow them to remain complacent nor apathetic. James, like so many other young champions, longs for intimate fellowship with the Lord and His empowering presence.

His new book is an outline in that journey that will help facilitate many others on their quest to know the Lord and participate in His harvest. I was truly blessed when reading his book to discover the depth of understanding the Lord has placed within James and the keys and secrets that will help catapult many others into the secret place with God. Like a proud father, I wholeheartedly recommend *Revival Hunger* and believe it will function like a key to unlock Heaven's resources to facilitate this last-day harvest.

Paul Keith Davis
Founder, WhiteDove Ministries

CONTENTS

FOREWORD

This book, *Revival Hunger* by Pastor James Levesque, was refreshing to me. As I read through it, I thought to myself, *Thank You, Jesus! Another generation is being raised up, speaking the truth in love and with power! I have great hope for the future.*

James Levesque's unique, raw insights into the very mechanics of revival echo my observations of the past 30-plus years of ministry. The prophetic word throughout this book is a clarion call by the Spirit of God to a generation that is hungry to get hungry for the "real."

I have been handed many books on revival over the years, and it's totally refreshing to see something that speaks with clarity into the subject of revival. Revival does not mean "anything goes"; revival means the Word of God is made plain and comes alive. No fables, no myths, no old wives' tales, no itching ears to be tickled. It is bold preaching and teaching of the Word of God, bringing about eternal results.

James Levesque has done just that. His simple yet profound message is proof that the Holy Spirit is raising him up as a voice to a generation that has totally lost its way. James and His precious wife, Debbie, are a new breed that God is raising up, along with their awesome church in New London, Connecticut.

We see the fire in both of them and it is reflected in this book. As you read it prayerfully, may a new hunger be stirred in your life as never before. Allow the Word and the Holy Spirit to strip away everything of the flesh and the soul, and get hungry for the real things of Heaven.

In James and Debbie we see the makings of a shaking that will spread across New England and the United States and to the nations. We salute you James and Debbie, and we say, "The best is yet to come." Thank you for being hungry for the real when so many are eating spiritual junk food in this hour. We love you dearly.

Dr. Rodney M. Howard-Browne
Missionary to America
Revival Ministries International
The River at Tampa Bay Church
Tampa, Florida

INTRODUCTION

We are living in the greatest hour the Church has ever known. However, there is so much compromise, and many are satisfied with less than Jesus intended for His people, producing a lukewarm Christianity.

God is empowering a generation (of all ages) to walk in divine power and purpose like never before. *Revival Hunger* is a call back to radical Christianity and an invitation to a supernatural life without borders!

Chapter 1

REVIVAL HUNGER

Finding the Substance of God Among the Fluff and Hype

What one generation is willing to tolerate,
the next generation will embrace. –John Wesley

A few years ago, during our normal Sunday morning worship service, one of our church leaders approached me. He told me that he had a vision to share with the rest of the congregation. I was actually quite shocked because he was not prone to seeing visions, and I had not heard him share before. Turning to him, I asked, "What have you seen?"

He replied, "Well, I saw a head floating around the room; it was Jesus' head!"

At that point I said, "Thank you," and turned around to resume corporate worship. I had no intention of letting him continue to share his vision with me, let alone with our congregation. It just sounded too strange to me to be biblical.

Seconds later, I felt a tap on my shoulder. It was the same man trying to get my attention. "Yes?" I said, a bit exasperated.

"Do you care to know what the head was saying?" he asked.

"Sure," I said, almost rolling my eyes.

"Well," he said, "As the head was floating around the room, it was saying one thing: '*I want My Body back!*'"

I was speechless as well as humbled. I immediately repented for cutting the man off, stopped the service, and had the vision shared from the pulpit. What followed was amazing! People responded to the message and were changed.

In being judgmental of this somewhat odd vision, I had nearly missed the message that Jesus was, in fact, interrupting *our* meeting to call *His* Body back to Him.

The vision was timelier than even I realized when it was being shared. We are in an urgent hour; modern Christianity is at a crossroads. A majority of the Church is settling for fluff, hype, fabricated testimonies, and fleshly desires instead of the true presence of God.

Many of us began with a pure desire to live life supernaturally but have settled for a life lived with little power or anointing. We have severed ourselves from the life source and headship of Jesus Christ and have given our lives over to fruitless, exhausting Christianity.

We settle for less-than and not-enough, addicted to ourselves instead of the cross of Christ. There's not a whole lot of talk about the price of following Christ. Long gone is the message of the cross and the call to deny ourselves daily.

We see few salvation experiences and even fewer healings in our normal, everyday lives. The true glory of God is barely present in our meetings. The Body of Christ has a nickel in its hand and is calling it a million bucks! We have jumped an inch off the ground and are calling it flying. We must see what we have become and cry out for forgiveness. Lord, help us!

The truth of the matter is that what we call powerful is really only Christianity 101 by the Word of God standard. We've only seen but a glimpse of the full expression of the gifts of the Spirit. In order to graduate from 101 to 201 and beyond, we must be willing to quickly answer the call to be totally His.

> We have severed ourselves from the life source and headship of Jesus Christ and have given our lives over to fruitless, exhausting Christianity.

I Give My All to Jesus

Jesus spoke some powerful words in Luke 9:23: *"Then He said to them* **all,** *'If anyone desires to come after Me, let him deny himself, and take up his cross daily, and follow* **Me.'"**

These words beckon us to follow Him all day, every day, forever. This call goes way beyond a one-time experience at an altar. A life lived for Christ is a constant surrendering of our wants and desires, killing them off, so that the purposes of God can be fulfilled through our lives.

In Luke chapter 5, Jesus approached a group of fishermen who clearly had no idea what was coming. Their decision, in that very pivotal moment, changed them and all of humanity forever.

> Do not be mistaken—
> revival will cost us
> everything!

Jesus charged them simply, "Follow Me," and they responded in the same simple way in which they were charged: *So when they had brought their boats to land, they forsook all and followed Him* (Luke 5:11).

A genuine encounter with God will compel you to forsake all earthly things and follow *Him!*

Several years ago, I was speaking to local church leaders in Loppersum, Holland, when in the middle of one of the meetings the Lord gave me a prophetic word for a certain young lady. After the meeting, while I was standing in the back of the church, she approached me. Despite the language barrier, she spoke these words as tears flowed down her face, "You speak strong to my heart." She threw her hands up in the air, still crying, and I will never, ever forget the words, in broken English, that came out of her mouth, "After hearing you, I give my all to Jesus!"

I give my all to Jesus! I was undone by her words! I smiled kindly, excused myself from the room, and ran to the bathroom. I locked myself in a stall and wept. I remember telling the Lord, "I will give everything to hear someone speak those words again!"

The desperately sincere words pouring from that girl's heart were the very heartbeat of God. *I give my all to Jesus.*

Do not be mistaken—revival will cost us everything! Nothing has changed. The Word is still the same today as it has been for over 2,000 years. Our cities, our nations, and this world will never be shaken by the power of God if believers are half-in/half-out. We must be an all-or-nothing people.

A Greater Measure

The Book of Ephesians speaks about the fullness of God, *"To know the love of Christ which passes knowledge, that you may be filled with all the fullness of God"* (Eph. 3:19).

The word *fullness* in this passage can be interpreted as "full measure." This implies that there are different measures of God available to us. God does not show favoritism, but we do receive measures of the Spirit based on our desire for Him.

If you don't believe that, just look around you. Most of us are flat-out bored because of a lack of anointing. If everything we have seen in the Body of Christ at this very moment is the full expression of Heaven, we are in trouble.

The Kingdom of Heaven is at hand. Jesus has been telling us that from the moment He arrived on earth in the flesh (see Matt. 4:17). These are the days of His power and His love. The time is now to hunger and thirst for righteousness.

Jesus said, *"Blessed are those who hunger and thirst for righteousness, for they shall be filled"* (Matt. 5:6). And in the Book of James, the Bible says, *"Draw near to God and He will draw near to you..."* (James 4:8).

> You can have as much of God as you want in this hour.

The initiation of this relationship begins with us here on earth, not in Heaven. As you and I draw near to God, He will draw near to us. When we hunger and thirst, then we will be filled.

In Genesis, we again see that earth touching Heaven is truly Heaven's heartbeat. *"Then he dreamed, and behold, a ladder was set up on the earth, and its top reached to heaven..."* (Gen. 28:12).

The ladder was set up on earth reaching toward Heaven. We are at the beginning of this process. We are the ignition on earth for the fire of Heaven. Look past the pull to compromise, and press in to Heaven!

Hunger triggered by a people seeking after the Lord will bring about an earth-shaking movement of God. This is the hour for the desperate to rise up and take their places!

You can have as much of God as you want in this hour. Will you die to who you are so that He may live?

The Coming Wind

By James Levesque 10/08/10

There is a wind; a change will blow.
God is choosing where it will go.
Filled with Heaven, the Ancient of Days
Will bury hype and man-made ways.

Sons of the Kingdom, a burning flame,
Word and Spirit lifting His name.
Outpouring and revival don't have to be said
For Jesus to come and resurrect the dead.

There is no room for manufactured revival,
Demonic doctrine that's outside the Bible.
The Church is hurting and full of sin.
We're called to cast devils out, not counsel them.

We've been manipulated for money; our hearts are strained
By slick talking men, who say they're ordained.
In spite of us, God is about to break through
Confound our minds, and bring in the new.

Points to Ponder

1. In what ways have you settled for hype and fluff in your faith? What does your heart desire in these areas?

2. What does it look like for you to give your all for Jesus?

3. Have you ever had an encounter with God that changed you? What happened?

4. What practical things can you do to press in to Heaven for a great measure of God's fullness?

Chapter 2

INTIMACY

God's Call to Come Near

Intimacy is a word that is thrown around frequently within American Christianity. Its actual meaning, however, is increasingly difficult to nail down. Some say that intimacy is prayer; others say that it is worship; while still others define intimacy with the Lord as attending a local church.

The word *intimacy* and the phrase *intimacy with God* can mean many different things to many different people. Yet for all our perceived interpretations, there still seems to be little evidence of true intimacy with the Lord within the Church.

We attend one good meeting after another, yet we continue to go home unchanged. Thousands of conference attendees hope to finally hit the spiritual jackpot, but after the fanfare wears off, they find themselves just as empty and disappointed as before. One thing never seems to change—our level of devotion to God.

Intimacy with the Father is complete devotion to Him. It is not about having a "works mentality" or striving to know the Father. It is about actually encountering Him. When we truly encounter God, we will never be the same again.

One Thing

David is one of the most noted men in the Bible. We read in the Book of Acts that David was a man after God's own heart (see Acts 13:22). No one else in Scripture is described as having such a heart.

> When we truly encounter God, we will never be the same again.

Acts 15:16 provides us with another of God's astonishing claims about David: *"After this I will return and will rebuild the tabernacle of David...."*

Why would God rebuild David's tabernacle? Why not Solomon's temple in all its splendor or the original tabernacle given to Moses by the hand of God Himself? The reason God chose David's tabernacle over the others is because David's tabernacle carried the heart of David.

Twice in the Scriptures, we see the phrase, *"the key of David."*

And to the angel of the church in Philadelphia write, "These things says He who is holy, He who is true, He who has the key of David, He who opens and no one shuts, and shuts and no one opens" (Revelation 3:7).

The key of the house of David I will lay on his shoulder; so he shall open, and no one shall shut; and he shall shut, and no one shall open (Isaiah 22:22).

What does that mean? What is the key of David?

It's way more than a cool worship song! To fully understand the key of David, we must look at the life that David lived. What better way to understand a man than to read the words spoken from his heart?

The Lord is my light and my salvation; whom shall I fear? The Lord is the strength of my life; of whom shall I be afraid? When the wicked came against me to eat up my flesh, my enemies and foes, they stumbled and fell. Though an army may encamp against me, my heart shall not fear; though war rise up against me, in this I will be confident. **One thing** *I have desired of the Lord, that will I seek...* (Psalm 27:1-4).

Wow! I'm not sure how many rough situations you have experienced, but David wrote these words in a time of battle and hardship unlike any we have ever seen. In the midst of what was potentially the greatest battle of his life, David said to the Father, "I want one thing."

I can just hear the Lord whispering to David as David wrote these words. "What is it, David? Do you want more troops? More weapons? What is it that you want more than anything else?"

David's reply is shocking in the best kind of way:

...That I may dwell in the house of the Lord all the days of my life, to behold the beauty of the Lord, and to inquire in His temple (Psalm 27:4).

In the midst of David's greatest battle, the one thing he truly desired was to behold the beauty of God. David clearly knew the value of intimacy. He knew that no matter what, if he could just catch a glimpse of the very glory of God, he would be triumphant in the battle.

Imagine going through the worst struggle of your life with that sort of mindset. Imagine knowing without a shadow of a doubt that if all you could do was see the Master's face, you would be set free! Imagine only wanting to worship Him.

Studying these words, we can see why the Lord spoke so highly of David. David desired to be near Him!

It's time for the Father to unveil Davidic worship again. Too many worship leaders have allowed arrogance to pollute the presence of God. Worship should be an outward expression of an already long-present inward cry.

Some of the most powerful times of worship the Church has ever experienced have been when a worship leader allows people to participate as if it is just them and Jesus—as if no one else is even in the room.

Let's get back to the man David was, and still is, through the eternity of the words the Lord gave him to share with us.

As the deer pants for the water brooks, so pants my soul for You, O God (Psalm 42:1).

How lovely is Your tabernacle, O Lord of hosts! My soul longs, yes, even faints for the courts of the Lord; My heart and my flesh cry out for the living God (Psalm 84:1-2).

O God, You are my God; early will I seek You; my soul thirsts for You; my flesh longs for You in a dry and thirsty land where there is no water. So I have looked for You in the sanctuary, to see Your power and Your glory. Because Your lovingkindness is better than life, my lips shall praise You. Thus I will bless You while I live; I will lift up my hands in Your name (Psalm 63:1-4).

> He knew that no matter what, if he could just catch a glimpse of the very glory of God, he would be triumphant in the battle.

Finishing Strong

After reading about the life and writings of David, you begin to see his heart. He longed to know the Lord beyond the surface. He wanted to dig in deep and know Him intimately.

In John 4:23-24, Jesus said:

But the hour is coming, and now is, when the true worshippers will worship the Father in spirit and truth; for the Father is seeking such to worship Him. God is Spirit, and those who worship Him must worship Him in Spirit and truth.

Logically, if Jesus said we must worship Him in Spirit and in truth, then we know it must be possible to worship Him *not* in Spirit and *not* in truth. Many people have worldly desires and ambitions mixing and meddling in their worship experiences. We must simply long to get carried away in His love and His presence—nothing less and nothing more.

This proved to be powerful in David's life. In Acts 13:36, we read, *"For David, after he had served his own generation by the will of God, fell asleep, was buried with his Fathers..."* Another translation of the same Scripture reads: *"When David had served God's purpose in his own generation, he fell asleep..."* (NIV).

There is one thing that is for sure: many today are living beneath the level at which God has called them to live. Rarely do we see men and women of God fulfilling the Lord's perfect will for their lives.

When David went to be with the Lord, there was not another sermon or psalm he could have written. There was not another battle he was supposed to fight. When David went to be with the Lord, there was nothing else he needed to do for his generation!

What are God's purposes for our generation? God is looking for those who will believe Him for this generation. Jesus is not looking for ability; He's looking for availability! He's looking for those who are willing to answer the call and those who are willing to go!

We have to give all that we are for all that He is. We have become too familiar, too complacent, with a God we barely even know. We must understand that there are aspects of God that have not yet been revealed. We have only begun this journey into the miraculous.

I believe that First Samuel 3:1 is an accurate depiction of the state of the Western church. *"Now the boy Samuel ministered to the Lord before Eli. And the word of the Lord was rare in those days; there was no widespread revelation."*

> We must simply long to get carried away in His love and His presence— nothing less and nothing more.

Before we fully dive into this, we must understand that the fact that the Word says that the word of the Lord was rare in those days does not mean that the Lord was not speaking. The word of the Lord was rare because people were not listening.

As in the time of Eli, the word of the Lord is rare in this hour because we have closed our ears to the truth of God. God is speaking more clearly than He ever has, and frankly, we are not listening. There must be a generation, made up of people all ages, who will hear the genuine word of God. It is time to stop heeding our own doctrine and to start understanding and heeding the words of Jesus!

As the high priest, Eli technically had the responsibility of hearing the voice of the Lord. However, he also had some problems—sin problems with his two sons. These problems were continually swept under the rug despite God's warning.

The surest way to cut ourselves off from God is to allow the sin in our lives to remain unchecked. Sin becomes more and more obvious the bigger the platform or stage we're on. The presence of God will cause the cracks in our foundations to show publicly.

A People Deaf and Blind

Besides being deaf to the word of the Lord, the Scripture also says that Eli was blind (see 1 Sam. 3:2). Once again, there is a corrupt priesthood alive today that is blind to the things of God and deaf to the word of the Lord. Spirit-filled people of God do exist today, who are true fathers and mothers in the Spirit; however, there are not many (see 1 Cor. 4:15).

This lack of spiritual fathers and mothers is not because God hasn't called people to be spiritual parents. It is because many choose not to live the life required of a spiritual parent or to respond to the call of mentoring. If the precious people of God are led by blind, over-sated, sin-hiding, disobedient so-called people of God, how can we advance the Kingdom?

That, my friends, is why we have Samuels. In First Samuel 3, we find the boy as the Lord found him, lying in the presence of the Lord, guarding the lamp stand. Samuel was in the place of His presence (a place he had been for a long time) when God finally called to him (see 1 Sam. 3:4).

The Bible says that Samuel, the faithful, obedient son that he was, ran to Eli and said, *"Here I am, for you called me."* But Eli replied, *"I did not call; lie down again"* (see 1 Sam. 3:5).

Don't think for a second that Eli didn't know what was happening when Samuel came to him! Eli was a mess and he knew it. It's no big secret to us, as human beings, when we're not living for God and when our lives are a mess. No divine revelation is needed to know when we are out of God's will.

Eli sent Samuel back to lie down because he was getting nervous! He was probably begging for the Lord to speak to him. At this point, his only hope was to hold off this next generation a little longer. A disobedient generation can recognize that when the next generation hears God, the former generation will be replaced.

In defense of the faithful, I'm not saying that it is not possible to finish strong. God's plan is actually for the merging of the generations, for the mature and the young in the faith to run together. We are heading toward the days spoken of by the prophet Joel (see Joel 2:28-30). It's about all ages! There are parents in the faith who embrace the younger, less-experienced generation.

> God's plan is actually for the merging of the generations, for the mature and the young in the faith to run together.

God has blessed my wife and me with amazing fathers and mothers all around us. (You know who you are, and we love you!) Anyone who knows us knows that we honor and love the leaders in our lives. The truths I preach about honoring and respecting spiritual parents are standards I live by. I could go on forever about the people in my life whom I honor.

I once attended an "apostolic roundtable" meeting. I listened as leaders in the faith spoke about how the younger generation does not honor or submit to leadership. As the discussion came to a close, they asked me for my thoughts on the issue, likely because I was the only young man in the room. Looking around at those men, contemplating the lives they had lived and what they represented as leaders, I gave a reply that left many of them stunned.

I answered by saying, "With all due respect to the people in this room, I want to honor older men of God, but can you show me a life and a cause worth honoring?"

I was not coming from a rebellious place, friends. It's not about disrespect. It's about being tired of reading the Bible, seeing the standard set by those words, and then looking around and not seeing it in the lives of those who supposedly live by the Word. Where is the anointing? Where are the people of God with weight and authority behind their words? We live with a priesthood that, for most part, is Pentecostal by name alone.

It is important to also say that young people must learn these principles as well. We run from leader to leader looking for someone to accept our sin. Instead, we need to listen and obey the counsel of our leaders and, most importantly, of the Lord.

Samuel did honor and revere the leadership of Eli's life, however obviously invalid it was. The Bible says that each time Samuel heard the voice of the Lord, he went to Eli awaiting instruction. He went to Eli three times before Eli finally acknowledged that it was the Lord calling Samuel.

That third and last time Samuel must have walked away from Eli filled with excitement. As he lay back down near the lamp of God, he was likely thinking, *This is what I have longed for—to hear the voice of the Lord!*

God did speak to Samuel and raised him up to be a mighty priest and prophet. All along, as Samuel was positioned in the place of His presence content with the Lord Himself, God was preparing to give him a spiritual promotion.

Intimacy is being content with just the Lord, our faces being changed in His presence. We must have our lives filled with the oil of Heaven. This is crucial for this hour. Come face to face with Jesus!

> Intimacy is being content with just the Lord, our faces being changed in His presence.

Desperate for a Change

When I first gave my life to the Lord, I was so desperate for Jesus that I wanted to do anything I could to meet with Him. There were days when I would get on my face and cry out to Heaven for 13 hours at a time!

I immediately began attending a local church where I soaked up anything I could. If a prayer meeting was being held on Saturday night at 6:00, I would arrive at the church at 5:00 and not leave until 3:00 the following morning. I would go home to sleep for a few hours and then go right back to church.

After my radical born-again experience, my mom had the hardest time understanding why I wanted to spend all day in the house. I had always been such a social person, constantly spending time with people. However, when Jesus opened my eyes, nothing else mattered to me. Every weekend—and I mean *every* weekend—Rick (a mentor and now a leader at our church) and I would clear the whole weekend to be with God.

If there was a service happening, I wanted to be there. We would drive over five hours one way and then back every Friday night just to attend a service. Every week, without fail, Jesus met us in a beautiful way.

During that time, I got my hands on Benny Hinn's book *Good Morning, Holy Spirit*. It completely wrecked me; I was undone! I thought to myself, *If this Holy Spirit is a person, I must meet Him!* I knew at that point, no matter what it took, I had to meet the Holy Spirit personally. I realized the anointing of the Holy Ghost would be the most precious gift I would ever receive in my lifetime.

I woke up one morning, finished the book, and told the Lord, "I'm going to lock myself in a room all day and night until Your Holy Spirit meets with me."

I took my Bible and went into the bathroom—good thing the house had two bathrooms—locked myself in, and began to cry out to the Father. If there was a power and an intimacy that I had not yet encountered, I wanted it. No more dry Christianity; it was time to meet with God!

About 14 hours into my bathroom vigil, I sensed a wind blow into the room, and the presence of Jesus completely overwhelmed me. Tears flowed uncontrollably, and the Lord spoke things to me that changed me forever.

There is no specific method to "touch God." This is just my story. But I challenge you to get desperate and fall fully in love with Jesus. When you're in love, you do wild things!

The Word of God is full of promises just waiting to be unlocked. The key to that lock is intimacy. It is a hunger to know the Lord more than we long to know anything or anyone else. As long as we are satisfied with the little we have received, we deny ourselves access to the fullness of God.

We must have a deep desire to go after Jesus—like David, like Samuel. The only way we will unlock the heart of the Father is through a lifetime of face-to-face encounters with Him. The up-and-coming Davids and Samuels will not come from a certain age group, educational level, or denomination. They will be those willing to do whatever is required of them in order to touch the Father.

> Their lives are actually quite the opposite because the spiritual temperature of thermometer believers is determined by what goes on around them.

Step past the cares of this world and into God's heartbeat. Many people give more attention to the devil than they do to God. If there is a problem or a crisis they completely allow the enemy of their souls to take priority.

Many of us, the moment we hear the words *pressing in to Heaven*, we clench up and accuse people of striving. But if we ever meet Jesus, we realize there is no striving in that! When we fall completely in love with Him, everything changes. Our lives will never be the same!

Which One Are You?

There are two types of believers: thermostats and thermometers.

Thermometer believers live for God (and that's a stretch), go to church, and are well meaning. However, they seldom walk in victory. Their lives are actually quite the opposite because the spiritual temperature of thermometer believers is determined by what goes on around them. Much like a regular thermometer, the reading of their spiritual temperature is determined by external factors and influences. These people are moved by everything life brings them: bills, family problems, a dog bite on the ankle, whatever!

They are up or down depending on what happens in any given moment of any given day. If the surroundings are good, then that's what they read. If the surroundings are bad, then that's what they portray at the time. Although the bad circumstances seldom affect anyone else, thermometer believers are wrecked for the day, maybe even longer.

This type of believer rides up and down with the cares of the world. They have no freedom. Even the joy they exhibit is just temporary until the mail carrier comes and drops off a bill.

Their spiritual temperature is displayed on their faces. You can see them coming a mile away. They like to project their internal reactions to external influences for everyone around them. They generally do not see victory in their lives. They may live 20-something years with Jesus and still experience the same struggles.

On the other hand, we have the thermostat believers. Thermostat believers change the spiritual atmosphere wherever they go. Much like an actual thermostat, their spiritual temperature, which is burning hot for God, is felt by everyone around them.

These believers change spiritual climates. They do not let external situations determine their temperature. They are consistent. They know that Jesus is always victorious, and they live in that victory.

They pray for the sick and decree life over everyone they are with. People love being around thermostat believers because they are encouragers. They are low-maintenance, high-impact believers who radiate the love of God.

Because Jesus is in you, you are called to change the spiritual atmosphere around you! Begin with your house, then your city. After that, let God's light within you shine over regions and nations!

We must understand that we cannot be thermostat believers on our own. A much greater strength is required—a supernatural strength, which is the result of our intimacy with the Lord that changes us from the inside out. It is not superficial or shallow. It is deep, and it is wide.

You are about to enter into an extended season of intimacy with the Father that will bring about widespread awakenings to many regions. Deep calls unto deep! Shhhh! He is calling you now. Can you hear Him?

> Thermostat believers change the spiritual atmosphere wherever they go.

Points to Ponder

1. What does *intimacy with God* mean to you? How has it manifested in your life?

2. Is intimacy with God truly your "one thing" desire? In what ways can you deepen your desire for His presence?

3. What is God looking for in His children? How might that look in your life?

4. Are you a thermostat or a thermometer? Explain. In what ways can you become more of a thermostat?

Chapter 3

AUTHORITY

The Secret Weapon of Every Believer

If the devil is around, you'd better be the one doing the talking.
–F.F. Bosworth

If we as the Church could truly understand the authority we have, everything would change. We are beginning to witness a generation that is born in Zion. This generation has a desire for the supernatural. They desire healing and have an earnest heart to see miracles. However, they do not understand who they are or the gifts they have been given.

I am going to spend some time in the next few pages talking about what true biblical authority is and is not.

"...*the people were astonished at His teaching, for He taught them as one having authority, and not as the scribes*" (Matt. 7:28-29). Clearly something about Jesus' life separated Him from others. We must live the same way! Authority is something many people talk about but few actually possess. Authority is what pushes us from *desiring to walk* in God's calling for our lives to *actually walking* in that which God has called us to.

All Power and Authority

Jesus commissioned the disciples in the Gospel of Luke, saying, "As you go, I give you all power and authority" (see Luke 9:1). Jesus has given to us what He gave His disciples—*all* power and *all* authority.

The Greek word for *power* used in this passage is *dunamis*, which is translated, "dynamite power." The Greek word used for authority is *exousia*, which means, "to act in and operate under a higher power."

Many people want signs and wonders and healings and miracles—the *dunamis* power of God. We will not fully operate in the *dunamis* power of God without the *exousia* authority of God. There is a big difference.

Imagine, for a moment, a police officer standing in the middle of a deserted highway when suddenly a huge Mack truck comes barreling toward him. Let me ask you a question: Which one has more power, the officer or the truck? Obviously the truck has more power! No person can stand in the way of the strength and the power of a huge vehicle like that.

Now, let me ask you another question: If authority was exercised on that highway, which one would yield to the other?

The answer, of course, is that the officer has the authority to shut down the power of the truck.

The Spirit works in a similar way. True authority, when properly exercised, will override power. Authority gives us the government of Heaven behind us and allows us to govern by the laws of the Spirit.

> True authority, when properly exercised, will override power.

Romans 8:2 says: *"For the law of the Spirit of life in Christ Jesus has made me free from the law of sin and death."*

A law is a law. We all know we will face consequences if we are caught speeding down the highway. It is the same way in the Spirit. There are spiritual laws. The Word of God is the authority and guidebook that governs our lives.

Spiritual laws override the natural. Spiritual laws will also honor the earthly laws and fulfill them. This is a truth we must understand today. There is a lack of true godly authority being practiced, and authority *must* be exercised for it to produce any fruit. We have all authority, and the devil knows it! Therefore, he will try everything he can to test it.

Your Call Is His Call

If you only *think* you have all authority, it is going to be ineffective. God is looking for those who will exercise His gift of authority. Jesus said in John 20:21, *"Peace to you! As the Father has sent Me, I also send you."*

In the same manner and likeness of Jesus, you have been sent! When Jesus died on the cross, He forever opened up the veil of a victorious life. Jesus is sending you! He has put His Spirit in every believer without measure and has thus enabled you to have all authority.

For whom He foreknew, He also predestined to be conformed to the image of His Son, that He might be the firstborn among many brethren (Romans 8:29).

You are someone Christ foreknew. This Scripture is a beautiful promise to every believer. You have been conformed to the image of Christ. Your call is His call.

Walking out Justice

There is so much talk about justice in the Church. I believe in justice, and I believe in praying for our government and our nation. However, do we truly understand what biblical justice is?

The Bible says this concerning us, the servants of the Lord:

Behold! My servant whom I uphold, My Elect One in whom My soul delights! I have put My Spirit upon Him; He will bring forth justice to the Gentiles. He will not cry out, nor raise His voice, nor cause His voice to be heard in the street. A bruised reed He will not break, and smoking flax He will not quench; He will bring forth justice for truth. He will not fail nor be discouraged, till He has established justice in the earth… (Isaiah 42:1-4).

I believe we are called to bring justice to this earth. I also believe that in order to understand justice, we must first understand injustice.

Sickness is an injustice!
Disease is an injustice!
Sin and bondage are an injustice!

If I asked you what you believe injustice looks like, what would you say?

You may say that abortion is an injustice. And I would agree. You may say, "If someone took all of my money, that would be an injustice." Yes, I also **think that is a form of** injustice. You may even tell me that if you are unfairly treated, that is an injustice, and I would agree. But I'm telling you that sickness is an injustice! Disease is an injustice! Sin and bondage are an injustice! Depression is an injustice! We need to shift our understanding of what injustice truly is so that we, as the people of God, can fill the need to bring justice to this world.

We must be agents of deliverance. We must be men and women who walk in the authority given to us by the Lord Jesus so we can bring about Heaven's will on earth.

I recently watched a disturbing news interview. This was during a politically charged season in the United States of America. This was especially true in California with Proposition 8 (a ballot measure stating, "Only marriage between a man and a woman is valid or recognized in California") under scrutiny. During the interview, a reverend was speaking on the issues at hand, and the hosts introduced a homosexual man to debate with him. Of course, the television networks need to cause some sort of argument to keep their ratings high, and they got what they needed by interviewing these two men.

First the reverend spoke. He began to ramble on about how homosexuality is a sin and an abomination to God. He spoke about how God hates this lifestyle and how this man is contributing to the moral decline of society.

Then the homosexual man jumped into the conversation and began to attack Christianity, God, and the Bible. He made numerous accusations concerning the Church and its lack of relevance and its abundance of hypocrisy.

> We are not bringing the justice of God to anyone if nobody gets changed, healed, or delivered!

The interview continued in this way, going back and forth about three times. It even elevated to a screaming match at one point. I was sick to my stomach just watching it. I began to think about what

I, and millions of other Americans, were witnessing. The whole thing was disheartening.

I'm sure that minister went home to a church full of high-fives and hugs. People most likely told him how bold they thought he was and what a great job he did standing up for God. He probably received all the "attaboys" a person can possibly receive. Meanwhile, the homosexual man went home without an encounter from Heaven.

Friends of mine, we are not bringing the justice of God to anyone if nobody gets changed, healed, or delivered! I am concerned about all these protests and marches where no one is set free or changed. Jesus went about doing good and healing, not condemning without action. We at least need to make an attempt! We are living in a generation that has learned to live a Christian life with no power. We try to find things to keep us excited because we have a lack of anointing and, quite honestly, because we are bored.

Really, What Would Jesus Do?

We need to stop living as if Jesus did not die on the cross. If we are truly going to bring justice in this hour, we need to begin to believe the Word of God and start casting out devils (see Mark 16:17). It cannot be anything else! Our nation and our churches are in moral decline. Many ministers are acting crazy and giving in to every fleshly desire, and the world is not getting any better!

If Jesus were standing here on this earth today, would He heal the sick? Or would He do everything but? Remember those *WWJD* (What Would Jesus Do?) bracelets? I saw thousands of people wearing a wristband but never praying for the sick. I observed people wearing the T-shirt but never getting rid of the sin in their lives.

We have a mandate from God to heal the sick. If we aren't witnessing many healings, we had better start praying for as many sick people as we can. The Word of God is always above this natural world. We must be tools of change. What does it matter if we march, shout, or wear tape if nobody gets saved? Where are the soul winners? Are we more concerned with worldly affairs than with godly affairs? The answer is obvious.

My wife and I were leaving a meeting when we found out that Michael Jackson had passed away. Now that was a shocker to me! It's tragic to have anyone die at 50. In the surprise of the moment, like most of America, we were on our phones texting everybody immediately. Then the Lord spoke to my wife. He said, "You are so diligent in telling everybody that some man died, but why aren't you as passionate about telling everyone that Jesus lives?"

Man! We repented in the car and told the Lord we want to make Him known everywhere we go. We must have a passion to see people saved, delivered, and healed!

I Had to Go Back

When we started our first church, we would go out on the streets of New London, Connecticut, and pray for the sick. One night we were on the pier praying for people, and a certain man caught my eye. I glanced at him and noticed one of his hands was hidden in his coat. I didn't receive a word from the Lord or anything like that; I just asked him, "What's wrong with your arm?"

The man then revealed his arm, and we could see it was withered. He explained that he had been in an accident 25 years earlier. He told us he was cutting down melons with his brother when his brother swung the machete and cut his arm. It was completely drawn up to his chest, twisted and cramped. He could not move it at all.

I, of course, asked him if we could pray for him, as we had seen many miracles on the streets, and I began to build his faith with the testimonies of these miracles. As I began to pray, people began to crowd around. They seemed to be coming from every direction. It was a crazy distraction, and I was nervous. So I finished my prayer quickly and said, "Thanks, man, we will keep you in prayer."

As we walked away, I was bummed. I couldn't believe that I was fearful. I had never felt that way in the streets before. We walked a little farther, and I felt the Lord saying to me, "You need to go pray again. You didn't exercise the authority I have given you."

To be honest, I had every reason to not pray for that man again. I tried to clear my conscience by telling myself, *But I already did it, Lord.* I could have come up with multiple excuses. In the end, however, I could not ignore the voice of the Lord. So, I told the people with me that we had to go back and pray for the man again. They looked at me as if I was crazy!

When we arrived back on the pier, I said to that man, "I would like to pray for you again because if Jesus was standing here you would be healed."

> I pulled his withered arm from where it was inside his coat. It fully extended—a complete healing!

He said, "OK."

I began to walk in the very authority I knew God has given each of us. I cursed every spirit of infirmity and commanded the man's arm to grow out in the name of Jesus. I finished the prayer, saying, "I command it *now*," and as I said those words, I pulled his withered arm from where it was inside his coat. It fully extended—a complete healing!

His family was astonished, and we witnessed everyone on that pier give their hearts to Christ that night. Even today, when we are walking in New London, that man will scream to get my attention, waving his arm in the air to show me he is still healed!

Choosing Authority

The Lord showed me that night that we always have a choice as to whether we want to walk in authority or not walk in authority. We can choose to neglect the voice of God and the needs of humanity, or we can answer God's call. It is not a matter of whether the price has been paid or not; it is a matter of whether we believe it or not.

I do not feel that we have a responsibility to perform miracles and healings. I feel that we have a responsibility to give Jesus a chance to do these things. Many people will not step out and believe Jesus because they have prayed for people in the past, and those people did not experience healing for whatever reason.

I refuse to live my life outside the Word of God. We need to live and walk in what has already been given to us. When Jesus rose from the dead, it was finished. We can now live a victorious life in Christ that we never knew was possible.

You cannot let the world tell you what God is saying. You are to tell the world what the Word of the Lord is saying! Walking in God's authority is to live and move in Him constantly.

The authority we've been given must be exercised, but secondly, and just as importantly, walking in authority requires submission. This is by far the most difficult concept for believers to accept. When we read the Gospels, we see that Jesus only gave full authority to those who were closest to Him. It is no different today. The ability to fully embrace authority requires a deep relationship with Christ. Jesus does not hold back blessings or favor certain people over others. As we draw closer to Him, more of our old nature dies, and we can more fully accept and embrace Jesus, which releases true authority in and through us.

I used to work at Tim Horton's, where I managed three restaurants and oversaw 40-plus employees. I was in charge of hiring, firing, salaries, all monies, and the day-to-day operations of the restaurants.

I worked hard and was recognized for it. I loved the job at the time, and although I didn't have an education, I was a willing worker and had a strong work ethic. The company saw the potential in training me and sent me to countless seminars and retreats so I could learn the ins and outs of the business.

I read book after book on leadership and business, and I often thought creatively about how to help the company grow. A relationship and trust was built between that company and me. It took time to build that level of trust and relationship.

During that season of my life, some things were certain. You may have had more education than I had and your resumé may have been ten times longer than mine. You could also have owned 500 other establishments and even created the very cash drawer I used to put the money in. But the simple truth was, if you came into my store and put your hand in my cash drawer without my permission, you would be arrested. There were no exceptions. You did not arbitrarily build the trust and the relationship required to do something like that.

Today, there are so many believers who want authority without relationship. The Bible is filled with promises that say things like, "...I will...heal their land," but it also says, "If My people...seek My face, and turn from their wicked ways..." (2

> The ability to fully embrace authority requires a deep relationship with Christ.

Chron. 7:14). Every promise in the Word of God is an invitation. Every prophetic word a believer receives is simply an invitation to step into those promises. But there must be a face-to-face relationship with God in order to bring about full authority. We cannot be part-time believers and expect full-time benefits.

Full-Time Believers

At my Tim Horton's stores, if an employee worked 35 hours a week or more, they received full-time benefits. If they worked under 35 hours a week, they were not eligible for those benefits. This was not because I didn't want them to have the benefits; it was simply because they did not work the hours required to receive full-time benefits.

If an employee told me that he wanted full-time benefits, but he had only worked 15 hours one week because he just didn't come in to work, it was no big deal at first. But if the pattern continued, that employee was no longer eligible to receive full-time benefits because he was no longer living a full-time benefits lifestyle at work.

> The law of the Spirit is waiting for someone to enforce it.

Jesus is looking for full-time believers. He's looking for men and women who are willing to do what it takes to break through. We cannot have a Pentecost with no cost! We cannot keep asking for everything but refusing to give anything in return. We must have a desire and a willingness to draw closer to God than ever before. A committed relationship with Christ is what we need.

We will receive an increase of authority as we break away from all of the distractions and press in to His heart. We must be willing to believe the promise of the Word over all natural circumstances. The law of the Spirit is waiting for someone to enforce it.

We already have the authority within us, and our ability to stand in it will increase as we look to Jesus. We need to understand that when Jesus was baptized, something changed.

When He had been baptized, Jesus came up immediately from the water; and behold, the heavens were opened to Him, and He saw the Spirit of God descending like a dove and alighting upon Him. And suddenly a voice came from heaven, saying, "This is My beloved Son, in whom I am well pleased" (Matthew 3:16-17).

When Jesus was baptized, the heavens were opened, and they have not shut! "Open heavens" are a real thing, but we need to understand that the heavens never close. Instead, it is the heads and hearts of the people that close. I believe that we can see an atmosphere of "open heavens" all day, every day. It is our inheritance as sons and daughters of the King.

If you are not seeing the fullness of Heaven invade your life, it is time to reposition your spirit and draw nearer to God than ever before. This is your promise. The Kingdom of Heaven is at hand! Jesus is looking for those whom He can commission into service to all humanity. They will be those who are willing to exercise the authority God has given them. They will be those who are willing to become so hungry for God in this hour that nothing else matters but Jesus.

We have experienced all the plans and ways of people. It is time for the ways of God! We don't need another method. We don't need another dead service. We need a fresh encounter with Jesus so His thoughts and desires become our thoughts and desires. We have to start seeing what He sees and feeling what He feels.

I invite you into a life where you can have all authority and power, a life where you are exercising the laws of the Spirit on a daily basis, a life where you draw closer to the Father and more of Him is revealed in you. Get ready for a life of victory and purpose. Come on!

> We can see an atmosphere of "open heavens" all day, every day. It is our inheritance as sons and daughters of the King.

Points to Ponder

1. Explain the difference between power and authority in your own words. Have you ever met someone displaying true spiritual authority? How were they different than you?

2. What sorts of injustice have you experienced? What is Jesus' solution for those problems?

3. How often do you see sick people get better when you pray? How often do you lead people to the Lord? Are you willing to take the risk and step out to do what the Word of God says in these areas?

4. What is your attitude toward submission to authority? How may this have affected your walk with Christ and your effectiveness in ministry to others?

Chapter 4

OBEDIENCE

The Key to Complete Favor

In front of every believer is a chessboard. We sit on one side of the board and the Lord Jesus Christ sits on the other. A lifelong scrimmage takes place at this chessboard. The game begins the moment we become born again, and it stretches right on through eternity.

Jesus makes the first move, and just like in any average game of chess, we make the next move. Then the Lord moves, and so on and so forth. Most of us begin this amazing life with the Lord and right away Jesus moves. Then, He asks us to make a move—any move to whatever degree.

When I became a Christian my relationship with the Lord began. I remember Jesus asking me to go to church on Wednesdays and Sundays. At the time, this was a stretch for me, but I listened. Every time I went to church, He would meet me there.

This was the small beginning of a wonderful journey of obedience to the King.

> If you want to move forward in the Spirit of God, you need to do the last thing He asked you to do.

Not too long after that, the church began a Saturday night class about the Holy Spirit, and the Lord impressed on my heart that I should go. Honestly, I thought to myself, *Three times a week in church? Really?* In the end I listened, and every time I went to the class, I encountered the Lord.

One night, as I was going to bed, the Lord began to speak to me about getting rid of all my secular music. He wanted me to begin to fill my life and mind with godly things. I already knew, at that point, that when the Lord asks me to do something, I should listen. Through obedience to the Lord's urging, I began to see an increase in His presence and power in my life. Every time I made my "move" of obedience to God, the Kingdom and glory would increase in my life.

How God Moves

When someone gave me the Word of God, I tried my best to obey it. Despite the opinion of others, I was determined to listen to Jesus and do what He asked me to do.

As I read the Word, I realized that Jesus gave us power to pray for the sick, and I knew, because of my previous experiences, that Jesus would move if and when I did. One of the problems with many believers is that they start this incredible life with Christ and immediately begin to build a pattern of not obeying, not heeding God's direction.

People wonder why they do not see God move in their lives when most of the time it's the result of a lack of obedience. If you want to move forward in the Spirit of God, you need to do the last thing He asked you to do.

We must not take the voice of God lightly. Every time we feel the unction of God, every time we feel the Lord asking us to pay for the groceries of the lady in front of us in the checkout line, we must respond.

Each time we ignore the voice of the Lord, we desensitize ourselves to the Holy Spirit. Just as it is possible to go from glory to glory in the Spirit and build a life of victory, we can also build a pattern of disobedience and barrenness.

In the Book of Hebrews, the Bible tells us: *"Though He was a Son, yet He learned obedience by the things which He suffered"* (Heb. 5:8). Even Jesus had to learn obedience! If that's the case, we must expect to learn also.

In my early 20s, I had an extreme hunger for God that could not be quenched. I would read, pray, and cry out to God for revival in New England. I didn't have great conferences around me. I didn't have many examples of great people of God. But I had the Word of God.

The more I read the Word, the more my hunger increased. I began to believe in greater glory. I promise you, I would not be a candidate for ministry in the eyes of most people. I definitely would not fit the typical mold of a "man of God." But I have always known that God doesn't call the qualified—He qualifies the called.

Growing up without my father and with a mother who was born deaf, then dropping out of high school and having a child at the age of 16 didn't exactly make me the kind of person most people would expect to see God use. But I had a hunger in me nothing or no one could satisfy. Then someone handed me a Bible and the secret was out. There was more to my life than what I saw around me! There was more than what anybody could imagine! I read the Word and believed it.

A Baked Potato and a Pork Chop

One night I was in my house praying and crying out to God for awakening and revival when I sensed the Lord asking me a question. "James," He said, "if you could do anything through Me and know you could not fail, what would you do?"

I was stunned. According to most of the people around me, I wasn't even qualified to lead a Bible study. But it wasn't people who were asking me this question, it was God! I immediately thought of William Booth, who once stated that if he could, he would "plant a church an inch away from hell." Come on!

I said to the Lord, "If I could, I would plant a church in this same city where I have known pain, where people have been murdered and poverty stricken."

After giving my answer, I took a few minutes to ponder why God would put that question in my heart. I even doubted that God would speak to me at all! It was so different from the views and opinions of the people around me, but it was so real. As I contemplated what God could be up to, I began to envision what could happen in the next five years or so in New England. In the middle of this open-eye vision, I heard a small voice say, "Let's do it."

Are you kidding me? I thought. God could not be asking me to do such a great task in this city. Surely there were more gifted folks in the area that He could use. I could not fathom that this was truly the voice of the Lord.

Then, I heard it again. "Let's do it."

I was stunned. I was watching the dreams of my heart unfold before my eyes. I knew that this would begin an amazing journey. Could it be that God was giving me the desires of my heart?

As I got up from prayer, I went to the fridge. As my hand touched the handle on the door, I heard this: "The key to slaying a giant is not a slingshot and stone. The key to slaying a giant is to use what is in your hands."

Wow! David killed the giant with what he had at hand. I fully believe that if David had a straw and a pea, he would have pea-shot the giant down. It is apparent that God wants to use what is in our hands. I did not have a lot to offer. You probably have more in your "hands" than I had in mine at the time.

In the mostly empty fridge, I saw a half-eaten baked potato and a pork chop that had been sitting there for a while. What is in my hands? I may not have a lot to give, but if David used a slingshot, then I have something to offer! I looked at that food and a thought hit me, *What if this is my stone? What could I do with this?*

It was a cold winter night in Connecticut, but I went for it. I heated the food, put on my coat and boots, and went outside. I walked past the parking garages where I knew the homeless would be on this winter night. I could smell urine, garbage, and just plain funk as I walked up the cement stairs at the back of the garage. On the fifth and final floor, I saw a man sleeping. He was curled up in a sleeping bag with a 40-ounce bottle of malt liquor close by.

> "The key to slaying a giant is not a slingshot and stone. The key to slaying a giant is to use what is in your hands."

I said, "Hey," to try to get his attention, but he was not

going to budge at all. So I kicked him lightly with my foot, hoping to awaken him and give him some food. He barely opened his eyes so I tried again.

"Hey." He quickly sat up, gathered himself, and looked very startled.

I said, "It's OK. I came to bring you dinner tonight."

He quickly perked up and took the plate. Staring at this man who was still looking at me as if I had three heads, I put my hand out and said, "Hey man, my name is James Levesque, and I am your new pastor."

Well, let's just say he hadn't heard that one before! He glared at me even harder and his eyebrows tilted in utter confusion. I told him that I was going to come down every night, Lord willing, and bring him dinner.

As I walked back into my house that night, I broke down and cried. It felt so good to listen to the Lord! I felt that I had finally touched the heart of God concerning this city.

If there is anything I have realized in the short amount of time I've been a believer, it is that not many people obey God. People have learned to ignore the nudge of the Holy Spirit, and eventually that results in a complete moral decline. Ultimately, it delays the awakening and true revival we say we desire to see.

Danger of Holding On

Disobedience is not a new problem! As you read the Word of God, you will see many circumstances in which people did not obey. Genesis records the earliest of these experiences.

The Lord shows up and calls Abram out to a new place.

Now the Lord had said to Abram: "Get out of your country, from your family and from your father's house, to a land that I will show you. I will make you a great nation; I will bless you and make your name great; and you shall be a blessing. I will bless those who bless you, and I will curse him who curses you; and in you all the families of the earth shall be blessed" (Genesis 12:1-3).

God's call was very simple and very clear—leave your family and go to a place I will show you. It was a clarion call to separate from the old and to step into a new land and a new destiny. This happens to many believers when God takes them to another place.

So Abram answers the call. Or does he? *"So Abram departed as the Lord had spoken to him, and Lot went with him…"* (Gen. 12:4). Wait a minute! What? Hold up! You're telling me that God called Abram out and told him to leave his family, and then Lot went with him? Then he didn't really leave his family. If Abram had left his family just as God had told him to, Lot would not have been with him.

Do you have a "Lot" to lose?

Abram essentially did what God called him to do, but he did it on his terms. If God told Abram to leave everything and everyone, that should have included Lot. This is the tragedy in the lives of many Christians today. They want to give God their all, but when He asks for it, they choose to do it on their terms.

We cannot continue to watch generation after generation say, "Yes, Lord, but...." There are too many "buts" in today's Church! Abram did not do exactly what God asked. And it is most certainly not by accident that he did not receive his promise until he was 100 years old! Was that God's perfect will? No one can ever really know. But it appears to not to have been God's original intention.

> In order for God to take us to the next level, we cannot bring any extra baggage with us.

Fast forward a few decades, after Abram had been renamed Abraham and his promised child had finally been given. The Lord makes another demand. He tells Abraham to sacrifice his only child—to sacrifice the very thing he had waited for. It was almost as if the Lord was asking Abraham to give up his promise just to get to the bottom of this obedience thing. In order for God to take us to the next level, we cannot bring any extra baggage with us. We must give everything over to the Lord.

We all know the story. Abraham was fully obedient the second time around, and God was faithful, providing a ram in the thicket (see Gen. 22:13). But this was Abraham's test to see if he would repeat the events of Genesis 12 or if he would give his all. Everyone has a "Lot" to lose.

Blind Spots

I heard Bishop T.D. Jakes say something powerful recently. He said, "In 28 years of ministry, I have come to a conclusion—the question is not, 'Are you blind?' but rather, 'Where are you blind?'"

This statement is so true! Every single one of us has blind spots, and we need to make sure that we are giving our all—being 100 percent obedient to what the Lord has called us to do.

Too many believers today only want to give God what they are comfortable giving and not what God is actually commanding. Because of their disobedience, many people live long lives that see more defeats than victories.

First Samuel 15:22 says, "...Behold, to obey is better than sacrifice, and to heed than the fat of rams." Many people can quote this verse, but most of us do not understand it.

The Lord had instructed Saul to wipe out an entire nation—men, women, children, animals, everything. Saul did what God told him to do, except for one little thing; he decided to take a few fatty rams home with him as a victory sacrifice to the Lord.

The Lord references this self-inflicted pious action in the above verse. What He is saying is that it would be better to heed His voice alone than to bring your "Lot" with you.

Saul's reasoning for his disobedience is found in verses 15 and 21 of the same chapter:

And Saul said, "They have brought them from the Amalekites; for the people spared the best of the sheep and of the oxen, to sacrifice to the Lord your God; and the rest we have utterly destroyed" (1 Samuel 15:15).

But the people took of the plunder, sheep and oxen, the best of the things which should have been utterly destroyed, to sacrifice to the Lord your God in Gilgal (1 Samuel 15:21).

Is seems like Saul was trying to somehow make his lack of complete obedience alright. It's never OK if we obey halfway! Saul had to pay a price for his lack of obedience.

I see an assembly of God rising up that will totally obey the voice of the Lord. Doors in the Spirit that have yet to be unlocked will be unlocked for those who fully obey. Just like Christ, we must learn obedience.

Many have asked me, over the few years I have been involved in ministry, "What's the secret? What is the key for walking in the power of the Spirit?" They probably do not want to hear my answer because I believe it has a lot to do with obedience.

Soon after I was born again, I started attending many different prayer gatherings, one of which was the pastor's 6:00 A.M. prayer meeting on Tuesday mornings. One Tuesday we finished prayer, and the pastor looked over at me and the other few guys who were still around and said something that shocked me at the time. "Do you realize how many people in this church have the call of God on their lives? These folks are sitting here week in and week out not pursuing the calling God has given them."

I remember going home totally shocked. I could not, at that point in my walk with God, understand how any believer could knowingly live beneath the place God had called them to serve or live.

Doors in the Spirit that have yet to be unlocked will be unlocked for those who fully obey.

After a quick talk with the pastor, I knew that was not going to be me. When I got back to my mom's house, I looked up to Heaven and I told the Lord, "Father, I would rather step out and believe You and fail than live my life and not obey You." It was a done deal in my heart. I was going to do all I could in this natural life to honor and obey the Lord.

We must be willing to listen to all God has to say and to step out no matter what the cost. As you and I continue to hunger and draw near to God, He will speak. The only question is will we listen?

Points to Ponder

1. What happens when you ignore God's voice? Have you ever experienced this in your life? What fruit did it bear?

2. What is the "Lot" in your life that you need to lose? What is the Lord calling you to do about it?

3. Have you ever made the choice to obey God, even when it was difficult or intimidating? What happened as a result?

4. Are you willing to live *beneath* the place where God has called you, or do you want His calling at any cost? What will you do today to walk out that choice?

Chapter 5

CHRIST IN YOU

The Hope of Glory Being Revealed

There is a second coming that will take place in every believer first.
–Dr. Brian Simmons

A teacher or a mother will look often look at a little child and ask, "Where does Jesus live?" We wait for the answer, almost able to speak it along with the child. It brings a smile to every person's face when the little child points to his or her chest and says, "In my heart." Yes, that always seems cute and wonderful. We all know that Jesus lives in our hearts. Isn't it funny, however, that as we grow older, we forget this simple truth?

This simple revelation is one that the Bride of Christ needs to understand before the coming of the Lord. We must have a revelation of Christ in us.

We see a number of promises in the Word concerning this fact. John 20:21 says, *"So Jesus said to them again, 'Peace to you!*

As the Father has sent Me, I also send you.'" In the same manner that Jesus was sent to this earth, we are sent to this earth. That, my friends, is a high calling. We also read in the Book of Romans:

> *But if the Spirit of Him who raised Jesus from the dead dwells in you, He who raised Christ from the dead will also give life to your mortal bodies through His Spirit who dwells in you* (Romans 8:11).

There is a distinct pattern forming. We have been sent in the same manner and likeness as the Father sent Christ, and the same Spirit that raised Christ from the dead lives in us! If these two scriptures were the only two scriptures left in the Book, we still would have been given more than enough to continue this life in faith. Every believer has resurrection power on the inside. But just because we know that it is *in* us does not mean that it will go *through* us. Many people today are familiar with this verse but do not live it. They are always looking to external sources when Jesus said the opposite.

> In the same manner that Jesus was sent to this earth, we are sent to this earth.

> *Once, having been asked by the Pharisees when the kingdom of God would come, Jesus replied, "The kingdom of God*

does not come with your careful observation, nor will people say, 'Here it is,' or 'There it is,' because the kingdom of God is within you" (Luke 17:20-21 NIV).

Before we can talk about the fullness of Heaven on earth, we need to understand that the unshakable Kingdom is within. This is a truth that the Church should thrive on but never really seems to grasp.

Fruitful Christianity

We need to really understand that all resurrection power already lives on the inside of us. Too many believers want everybody else to set them free. They want others to do all the work. Though there is some truth in what they desire, the author of Hebrews writes:

Therefore we also, since we are surrounded by so great a cloud of witnesses, let us lay aside every weight, and the sin which so easily ensnares us, and let us run with endurance the race that is set before us (Hebrews 12:1).

Yes, let us! There have been times in my life when I just decided to lay down the sin. I didn't have a huge mystical deliverance; I just experienced the strength of God in me. I am not negating the importance of prayer, deliverance, or inner healing. I'm just making a point.

You cannot access the fullness of Christ within without dying to self first. To truly allow Christ within you to be released outside of you, you must already be dead to your "self." In saying this, I am assuming that we understand it's all about Jesus. In no way do I feel that anyone, including myself, has anything to boast about in his or her own strength or ability. Jesus, through His grace and mercy alone, has opened this wonderful life up for us.

Jesus said that He came to give us "life and life more abundantly" (see John 10:10). When we look at the Body of Christ, do we see life and life more abundantly? Do we see the final expression of a great salvation? Do we know without a shadow of a doubt that Jesus lives?

I believe that unless we gain an understanding of the Christ who lives within us, we will continue down a path of fruitless Christianity. We have been given too great a gift within to let the full expression of that gift continue to lie dormant.

Joint Heirs

In the Book of Romans, the apostle Paul said:

The Spirit Himself bears witness with our spirit that we are children of God, and if children, then heirs—heirs of God and joint heirs with Christ, if indeed we suffer with Him, that we may also be glorified together (Romans 8:16-17).

We are not only His children but also joint heirs. An heir is someone who is given an inheritance from his or her Father. You are an heir with Christ, an equal heir with Christ. You are His expression on earth today. We constantly tell our church body,

> To truly allow Christ within you to be released outside of you, you must already be dead to your "self."

"You are the answer to revival and awakening in New England. It's you!" You will be a living, breathing revival walking around on two legs. If you had any more power, you would be a threat to the Trinity!

We must first understand who lives inside of us; then we will begin to live life a bit differently. The Bible says that we go from glory to glory:

> And we, who with unveiled faces all reflect the Lord's glory, are being transformed into His likeness with ever-increasing glory, which comes from the Lord, who is the Spirit (2 Corinthians 3:18 NIV).

I have found it very difficult to actually experience going from glory to glory. Many people who have experienced a powerful movement of God or hints of revival seem to get stuck in the moment. If God brought a revival in the 1980s, they get stuck in the mindset, ideologies, and truths of that era. I have watched various folk who have experienced God move. Many times people will try to recreate that same scenario. It's sad. It is going to take a violent hunger for revival today to bring about awakening.

We are a people who perpetually seek to marry methods. We need to get married to Him! We don't need another method; we need the ability to touch the heart of God in a moment of desperation. Smith Wigglesworth often said that the only thing he was satisfied in was the fact that he was never satisfied. Is this true for us?

There is an intimate, powerful union between the Lord and the Church that has only been seen in bits and pieces in the past. But it will become more common in the coming days. This awakening spirit will reveal the hope of glory in us.

> You will be a living, breathing revival walking around on two legs.

Oneness With Christ

When Jesus was facing His death, He uttered a very powerful, yet misunderstood, prayer. It is a prayer that I believe will have to be in the hearts and on the lips of every believer before Jesus returns.

I pray for them. I do not pray for the world but for those whom You have given Me, for they are Yours. And all

Mine are Yours, and Yours are Mine, and I am glorified in them (John 17:9-10).

Jesus is obviously praying for His disciples, the very people who walked with Him, the people whom He would infuse with His Holy Spirit here on earth. As Jesus prayed for His disciples, He also began to pray for us, the future generations of the children of God who would be touched by the power of the Holy Spirit. *"I do not pray for these alone, but also for those who will believe in Me through their word"* (John 17:20).

Jesus is clearly asking on our behalf! He included you and me in this historic prayer, His last great request on earth. He began by asking, *"That they all may be one, as You, the Father, are in Me, and I in You; that they also may be one in Us..."* (John 17:21).

Jesus is asking that we would be *one* just as He and the Father are *one!* Come on! Jesus and the Father are One! They are two-thirds of the Godhead. Jesus is asking that we would be one in Him and He in us! That is very powerful, yet, considering the standard today, many seem to find it hard to understand. Then Jesus clarified the reason and purpose for this great oneness: *"... that they also may be one in Us, that the world may believe that You sent Me"* (John 17:21).

We are the proof on earth that Jesus was actually sent here. The world is looking for proof that Jesus is real, looking for an assurance that the Gospel is power and truth. I believe God has purposed for us to be His proof and expression on earth today that Jesus is real.

In this prayer, Jesus is saying that the reason for this oneness is that the world may believe. Our lives must be a continual expression of the reality of God. We must, therefore, govern and guide our lives accordingly.

The Jesus Gauge

If what Jesus is saying is true, then what is our gauge here on earth? If the reality of Christ must be revealed in you, then according to the world around you, how real is Jesus? If your very life is the gauge, the meter of the resurrected Christ, how real is Jesus? Let me rephrase it this way: do those who know you know Jesus is real?

For years we have been taught to depend on everyone else. We have looked to pastors, worship leaders, counselors, and teachers for answers and insights, but we must be steadfast. We are the ones carrying this present glory.

Again Jesus encourages us to another level in John 17:22-23:

And the glory which You gave Me I have given them, that they may be one just as We are one: I in them, and You in Me; that they may be made perfect in one, and that the world may know that You have sent Me, and have loved them as You have loved Me.

The glory of Jesus has been given to us and is in us. We are just as much in Christ as He is in us. It is a perfect union, a Heaven-established union for the purpose of revealing the truth and reality of Jesus. This means we must adjust our mindsets and understanding. We have to begin to live our lives as if we have been given a heavenly mandate, as if Jesus lives on the inside of us. Christ is in us, and He *wants out!*

Bring the Sickest Person

On a trip to Ghana, West Africa, my team and I were participating in crusades with a lovely ministry there, having partnered with an amazing man of God. We held the crusades at night and helped

> Christ is in us,
> and He wants out!

out painting children's homes and assisting with other practical needs during the day. We had a few days open and decided to change up the schedule. Although I was thankful for the souls and miracles, I wanted to walk in the villages and meet the needs of the people of Ghana. Much like the example set by Jesus, I desired to walk among the sick and less fortunate. I wanted to release the Christ within.

So we woke up one morning and told our team we were going to walk into the villages and pray for the sick individually. We wanted to lead people to Christ and see His power touch the many who needed it. The team was a little freaked out; some were probably thinking, *I didn't sign up for this.* Nonetheless, prompted by the example Jesus set, we wanted to stretch everyone's faith and see souls saved and the sick healed.

Many people wanted to come with us, probably just to watch, but I only took three African pastors who could help with interpretation and ministry. We began our journey after praying with the team. In the first village we encountered, I approached the multitudes and screamed, "I want you to bring the sickest person in this village to me. Jesus is here, and He wants to heal everyone!"

Let me tell you, the pastors did not expect me to say that. So there I was waiting for them to interpret what I said, and they were just staring at me! It was the most awkward few moments, so I decided to scream it again, as if they hadn't heard me!

Finally, they interpreted my words, although I could sense they were a bit hesitant. It was a bold proclamation upon entering a village for the very first time. As they began to interpret my words, some people grabbed my hands and rushed me to a sick family member. Clearly I did not know what to expect. They took me to a man who must have been in his 50s and told me he had not been able to move his left side and had not worked for 17 years. He had been paralyzed and confined to a room for all of that time.

As I approached the bench-like bed he was lying on, the translators gave me the "here you go, James, this is what you

88

wanted, sir" look. A lot of people gathered around me as I looked at the man. Up to that point, I had not seen anyone get up from his or her deathbed. I was trying to do the most Pentecostal thing possible, thinking of John 5 with Jesus and the lame man, so I looked at the paralyzed man and said, "Do you want to get well?" I figured I could look super-spiritual and somehow put it off on him if things didn't go well.

The situation is funny looking back, but as it was happening, I was a bit nervous. The man quickly replied in his language, "What do you think?"

OK then. Got it, buddy! I thought. *I guess we need to give Jesus a shot.* As I stood over the man, this thought immediately came into my head, *If Jesus was here right now, what would He do?* Jesus would lay His hands on this man and speak to him to get off his deathbed! He would clearly say, "Rise up and walk!"

I fully realized at that moment that Jesus was there. He was inside of me. I thought, *When I lay my hands on this man, it is no different than if Jesus laid His hands on this man.* Of course, it was a little different because Jesus' physical hand is not my physical hand. But the Bible is clear that as far as power, anointing, and destiny, they are mine and they are yours!

So, as I laid my hands on the man, I had a picture of Jesus right there with me laying His hands on him too. At that moment, with the revelation of who was with me and in me, I said, "In the name of Jesus, I curse this spirit of infirmity, and I command life in his body now! In the name of Jesus Christ, rise up and walk! Get off this bed!" I watched as strength came upon the man, and he instantly jumped off his bed. Mobility came back into his body, and he began to shout, "Jesus is alive!"

> Releasing Christ's miracle power has everything to do with understanding what you and I have been given.

I grabbed his hand and walked him out to the courtyard where I had given the initial call to the sick. Everyone began coming out of their houses as they knew this man to be paralyzed and not able to walk.

As the crowds gathered, I got up on a milk crate and shared the Gospel. Many gave their hearts to Christ for the first time after seeing Jesus perform this miracle.

Releasing Christ's miracle power has everything to do with understanding what you and I have been given. If you can comprehend and receive Christ's desire for you on earth, I believe you will be empowered to do great things for the Kingdom.

This is one of the greatest hours to be alive. In the beginning of this chapter, I talked about John chapter 20 and Christ's call to send us out in the same manner in which He was sent out. The very next words that Jesus spoke were as follows: *"And when He had said this, He breathed on them, and said to them, 'Receive the Holy Spirit'"* (John 20:22). Why do you suppose Jesus had to say, *"Receive the Holy Spirit"* after he breathed on them? It is because it is possible for Jesus to be breathing and us yet we don't receive it.

Just because Jesus is moving in revival or desperately trying to release truths to His precious Church does not mean that we will receive any of it! It is possible for Christ to be moving and for us not to be open to Him. We must receive the Holy Ghost. We must position and reposition ourselves to receive His Holy Spirit. We have to relinquish our mindsets so that we can embrace the Father's desire to reveal who lives within us.

The Bible says, *"In Him we live and move and have our being..."* (Acts 17:28). That means everything we do is in Him! Life isn't life if we are making moves outside the will of God. Absolutely everything we do must be in Him. It is Jesus alone who will take our lives and make them meaningful for the Kingdom's cause.

Get ready to see the second coming on the inside of you. Jesus is waiting for the veil to be removed from your heart. Let Him in—*then let Him out!*

Points to Ponder

1. What does it mean to you that the Kingdom of Heaven is within you? Ask the Lord for a deeper revelation of this truth in your heart today.

2. Do you have persistent sin struggles or areas of unfruitfulness that you seem unable to overcome? How might the truth of Christ's power within help you find freedom?

3. How does it make you feel that you are an equal heir with Christ? In what ways do you live like an heir? What areas of your life need a greater revelation of this truth?

4. What does your life say to the people around you about the reality of Christ's truth and power? What can you do to improve?

Chapter 6

BREAKING BARRENNESS PART 1

Destroying Unbelief

In the Book of Isaiah, we see two somber accounts of the state of Israel, and I believe they are a prophetic picture of many saints in the Body today. The first is found in Isaiah 26:18:

We have been with child, we have been in pain; we have, as it were, brought forth wind; we have not accomplished any deliverance on the earth....

These folks in Judah remind me of so many Christians today. If anything can sum up much of what I have seen, it is a lot of over-promising and a lot of under-delivering. These were a people who walked around claiming one thing and having done another.

Too many believers have been to service after service but have not changed. They have received so many words that they are now like spiritual harlots and can't get enough. There is a lot of fluff and hype and not enough substance.

Many ministers exaggerate and make a lot out of a little fruit, as if the Holy Spirit isn't enough. The people referenced in Isaiah 26 were constantly saying they were carrying children, but when it came time to bear these children, they only brought forth wind. Wow! Sounds like many believers today.

> Too many believers have been to service after service but have not changed.

Lying testimonies and false words have opened the gate for more hype and flakes to emerge. To find real anointing in today's services is rare. There is not a lot of presence, but there are lots of presents. People long for the Gospel goodies, but no glory is attached to their empty words. Many who are walking around with crazy claims only seem to birth wind. Lord, help us all!

Believe the Hype?

Name-dropping has become way too common. Apostle this and that—what happened to true biblical power? My concern is that the bar has been so dropped that our grid for what is genuine and true is shallow. Meanwhile, we preach from a Bible we don't believe. Even people who claim to have "signs" like diamonds and gold dust have turned away from the face of Christ, and few are getting saved.

I have had people in my meetings plant gemstones in order to make others believe they appeared miraculously. Somehow they think God will let that go on! Surely not. Again, I believe God can do anything, but bring me a person who saw a diamond appear in a meeting and then sowed it into widows and orphans. That will be the testimony I will share.

We are becoming spiritually bored as a society, and now we are finding false fantasies to keep our attention. These things are not the power of Jesus. Where is the meeting where people are repenting of sin? I want to go to that meeting, or a meeting where all we do is cry out to God to save our cities and regions, where faith is built to step out and believe God for the impossible.

We do not need any more dead meetings. We don't need any more meetings where "gemstones" show up, yet everybody still goes home with devils. This does not produce true disciples. Where are the soul winners? Where are those who will find gems in people?

We cannot keep telling people that an "outpouring" is happening when we still have only 30 people and nobody is being saved. I recently saw an update on another minister's Website. He was telling everyone that the "fire" of God had hit and a true "outpouring" is taking place. Meanwhile, two-thirds of his Website's front page either asked for meetings or money. Come on, man. False claims like this dilute the real presence of God and the real meaning of revival. I pray for these ministers and I love them. I realize that many times they are doing this out of a genuine heart for revival. But false finish lines will always lead to destruction.

Why don't we let changed lives determine if something is a genuine revival? Long gone are the Welsh Revivals and the Great Awakenings, where people just let the glory do the speaking. Now we need television cameras, Facebook, and every other media to help fabricate a truth.

I believe God can use the media. He has in the past and will again. However, I do not feel the need to fabricate the power of God. Jesus is enough.

God is calling! He is looking for the real to emerge from the fabricated. There is an Isaiah 6 clear call going out. *"Also I heard the voice of the Lord, saying: 'Whom shall I send, and who will go for us?'…"* (Isa. 6:8).

This is the Word of the Lord today. However, not many answer this high calling in Christ. It is a call to live for the purposes of God, completely devoted to Him. The next verse demonstrates that there is an urgent reason for such sold-out sons and daughters to arise. *"…Go, and tell this people: 'Keep on hearing, but do not understand; keep on seeing, but do not perceive'"* (Isa. 6:9). This is a picture of many people's mindsets.

My wife and I travel all over the world, and as I write this, we are on a three-week trip to Nova Scotia, Canada. Every night we are witnessing salvation, deliverance, and healing. We love strengthening the churches and working with our family here. We love doing God's work.

But in many of the places we travel to, we see the same people spiritually stuck. I have watched people go from conference to conference and never change. I see the same intercessors struggling with the same old mindsets year after year.

> I do not feel the need to fabricate the power of God. Jesus is enough.

A crisis is happening. When many saints do not grow, there has to be a reason. I believe that spiritual barrenness is the crisis that is happening. God is speaking, but we are not changing. This is a cloak of unbelief, a hood covering the heads of God's people so they cannot experience breakthrough.

False Finish Lines

In the Gospel of Luke, we see a picture of false finish lines. The enemy places a false finish line in the way so we do not advance the Kingdom or achieve freedom.

About eight days after Jesus said this, He took Peter, John and James with Him and went up onto a mountain to pray. As He was praying, the appearance of His face changed, and His clothes became as bright as a flash of lightning. Two men, Moses and Elijah, appeared in glorious splendor, talking with Jesus. They spoke about His departure, which He was about to bring to fulfillment at Jerusalem. Peter and His companions were very sleepy, but when they became fully awake, they saw His glory and the two men standing with Him. As the men were leaving Jesus, Peter said to Him, "Master, it is good for us to be here. Let us put up three shelters—one for You, one for Moses and one for Elijah." (He did not know what he was saying.) While he was speaking, a cloud appeared and enveloped them, and they were afraid as they entered the cloud. A voice came from the cloud, saying, "This is My Son, whom I have chosen; listen to Him." When the voice had spoken, they found that Jesus was alone. The disciples kept this to themselves, and told no one at that time what they had seen (Luke 9:28-36 NIV).

At that time, this may have been the most amazing experience Peter had ever had. I'm sure he was thinking, *This is the greatest anointing I have ever seen!* He immediately wanted to build an altar at that place of encounter. God, the Father, basically rebuked him and told him to listen to and follow Jesus.

How many false finish lines are in our lives today? The hardest place to go is from glory to glory. Through our encounters and experiences we get caught up in yesterday's glory.

It amazes me how many "false finish lines" believers have stopped at throughout Church history. Look at the gift of tongues. Now this is a powerful gift. Paul said he speaks in tongues of men and angels (see 1 Cor. 13:1).

> The hardest place to go is from glory to glory. Through our encounters and experiences we get caught up in yesterday's glory.

However, when Jesus was commissioning the believers to tarry and wait in the upper room for the promise of the Father, He did not mention tongues! He told them they would receive power after the Holy Ghost came upon them, and they would be witnesses in Jerusalem, Judea, and the uttermost parts of the earth (see Acts 1:8). When the wind of Pentecost blew, tongues of fire appeared to the folks gathered in the upper room (see Acts 2:1-4). They did not realize what they were even waiting for. They only knew Jesus said the Holy Spirit would come upon them.

Throughout the years of Church history, we have witnessed God's Spirit and power move in amazing ways. During the Azusa Street Revival, tongues played a huge role in the infilling of the Holy Spirit. This still rings true today. However, even though the gift of tongues is a big part of our lives, many have fallen victim to the experience. I know many people who have tarried and believed God for "the baptism of the Holy Spirit," and when they received the gift of tongues, they stopped. Tongues? Jesus did not die on the cross just for tongues.

So now we have many who are Spirit-filled with the evidence of speaking in tongues, but they are not witnesses. They have no clear distinction of power from on high. Please know that in no way do I diminish the gift of tongues. I think it is so precious when it is received. I just believe that tongues are the starting point. When you and I are filled with the Holy Ghost, the door is opened. But we have to walk through it. We must continue in all the authority and power that is given to every believer. Tongues are a wonderful gift, but the enemy would love for the Church to stop there.

Just Shy of the Line

Satan does not need to get us to commit one of the "major sins." All he has to do is convince us to live beneath the place God has called us to live. If we settle for a life that is not filled with victory and freedom, we have not received God's best for us.

> "Hollywood" church stuff will not stand in the day of His power.

We have witnessed the creation of false finish lines many times and have gone through seasons when God has expressed a nature of Himself to us. When divine healing came, many people could not fathom that any more could be released.

I have seen the prophetic fall into the same trap. God wanted to release a prophetic understanding to the Body of Christ. However, I do not believe He meant for us to take the gift of the prophetic to the extreme, whereby people who hear God are themselves exalted.

In this natural life, we seem to be suffering from an identity crisis. We, as Christians, do not fully realize who we are, and somehow we exalt those on a platform or behind a keyboard. This "Hollywood" church stuff will not stand in the day of His power. God will always use media, but as long as people are being worshiped, the move of His Spirit will surely die.

I heard the story of a great man of God who was overseas. After a few weeks the crowds began to swell. At one point 100,000 people gathered. They met every day, and a nation was starting to change. However, God spoke to this man and told him to leave the nation because the people were starting to worship him and not Jesus. This made me wonder how many people in his shoes would have left the revival so that God could be glorified.

Some of the greatest examples Deb and I have as mentors and friends today are people whom God spoke to that, after a few weeks of ministry somewhere, would have to step out and step aside. They knew that their call was to light a fire and then see the church rise up. Wow! Many of my co-laborers (in my age group) want the exact opposite. They want meetings where they are ministering to go on for months so their names can be great. I'm telling you, Jesus will have none of that.

Dead Men Walking

A number of years ago, I was in prayer and I was asking God to live *big* inside of me, that my fleshly desires would not matter. I began to hear the Lord telling me that I would have to die to myself before He could live inside of me. I was not totally sure what He meant. But right after God had spoken to me, I turned on the television and watched two great healing evangelists talking. As I focused on what they were discussing, one of them said, "I remember the day I died." The other man of God said, "Me too. I can take you back to the place that I no longer lived." I watched as they talked about what it meant to "die daily." They spoke of how we must be dead to ourselves so that God can live through us here on earth.

Now, in no way am I saying that God wants you to die physically. I am clearly talking about a spiritual death that will manifest in this natural life.

After hearing their discussion, I turned off the television and began to cry. I wanted to die to my own nature and fleshly desires. I did not want James Levesque to live anymore. As I was crying, I heard the word of the Lord come to me: "James, you need to see your own funeral." *What did that mean? I need to see my own funeral?* Then I realized that I had to have a "funeral service" for James Levesque.

I ran to the bathroom, locked the door, and looked in the mirror. It was a Saturday morning, and I was about 15 years old and was facing some major problems in my life. As I looked in that mirror, with tears running down my face, I said, "God, I want to see myself die, so that You can live." I wanted God's purposes to be my purposes. I wanted to feel what He felt and see what He saw.

As I opened my eyes after saying that prayer, I looked in the mirror and saw an open-eye vision of my funeral. I could see a casket with flowers, and there was a sign on the coffin that said James Levesque. While I was watching this scene play out, I could sense the presence of God filling the room. I wanted so badly to live for Him and not for myself. I watched for about two minutes and felt the supernatural might fill the room. I knew that as I would seek the face of God, He would grant me the desires of my heart to live for Him!

When I put my hand on that doorknob, I knew that James could not live anymore. I knew that Jesus had to be the only one alive. My earthly desires did not matter. If you decide to live your life for the

> I realized that I had to have a "funeral service" for James Levesque.

purposes of God, you will never be the same again! Paul said in Galatians 2:20:

> *I have been crucified with Christ; it is no longer I who live,* **but** *Christ lives in me; and the life which I now live in the flesh I live by the faith in the Son of God, who loved me and gave Himself for me.*

Come on!

How Low Can You Go?

A friend of mine who leads worship once said in a song, "The Kingdom of God is the world in reverse." I believe that, but our worldly systems of growth and success have managed to creep into the Church.

Earlier I mentioned a secular music star who died a few years ago. Many thought he was the "King of Pop." I was in shock at how shrines were immediately built when the news of his death got out. Now, don't get me wrong. I'm OK with people grieving and mourning. Honestly, I have found myself praying for his family too. But this got me thinking about what the world considers success.

I do not believe that you have had a great life if you spent most of it in emotional bondage. See, the world looks at greatness much differently than the Lord looks at greatness. We are moved and impressed by cheers and great words from people. God is not moved by that.

The Bible tells us that the disciples came to Jesus with a powerful question, *"Who then is greatest in the kingdom of heaven?"* (Matt. 18:1). Jesus didn't miss a beat, and He pulled the most unlikely maneuver. He called a little child to Himself and began to answer the question. *"Assuredly I say unto you, unless you are converted* [change] *and become like little children, you will by no means enter the kingdom of heaven"* (Matt. 18:3).

Jesus told the disciples they had to change. The very ones who walked and talked with Him, who saw miracles and multitudes fed! Jesus looked at them and told them that unless they humbled themselves and changed, they would not be fit for the fullness of God.

That is pretty intense. We often look at increasing in the Spirit of God and think we can manipulate ourselves to a new level—as if Jesus doesn't see our selfish, worldly ambitions and motives. Too many people today want the call of God because they want crowds and media attention. Where are those who want to hide their lives and gifts behind Him?

The apostle Paul is a great example. On any given Sunday morning, many ministers will preach from his writings. Imagine writing something so powerful that thousands of years later people still read your writings and letters. As we read Paul's letters, we get a snapshot of many powerful things. One that can go unnoticed is Paul's personal growth. We read in Galatians 2:6:

> But from those who seemed to be something—whatever they were, it makes no difference to me; God shows personal favoritism to no man—for those who seemed to be something added nothing to me.

Paul, writing to the churches in this region, was facing a lot of criticism. His critics were claiming the Gospel Paul wrote was not the true Gospel. Many other accusations also rose up. In the first two chapters of this book, we see Paul addressing some of these issues right away. He then takes a hard stand and says, "These folks who think they are something, well, their message adds nothing to me!"

We witness Paul's writing again in First Corinthians 15:9, "For I am least of the apostles, who am not worthy to be called an apostle, because I persecuted the church of God."

We see a different example when Paul refers to himself. He says that he is the least of all the apostles. This is a small step away from saying, "Those who thought they were something, their message added nothing to me."

Then we see Paul addressing himself yet again in the Book of Ephesians. "To me, who am less than the least of all the saints, this grace was given, that I should preach among the Gentiles the unsearchable riches of Christ" (Eph. 3:8).

This is another example of Paul speaking of himself, but it is far from his fired-up response in Galatians and far from referring to himself as being the least of the apostles. He now refers to himself as the least of all the saints, the believers.

> If you and I advance in the Kingdom of Heaven, it will simply be because we have gone lower, not higher.

This is a powerful understanding because many of us believe that as we increase in the Kingdom, we somehow attain something. The truth is that if you and I advance in the Kingdom of Heaven, it will simply be because we have gone lower, not higher.

Even further, we see another claim by Paul about his life that seems to put everything into perspective. First Timothy 1:15 says: *"This is a faithful saying and worthy of all acceptance, that Christ Jesus came into the world to save sinners, of whom I am chief."*

Paul, the chief of sinners? This is yet again a different description of Paul the apostle. Here he tells his spiritual son in the faith that he is the chief of sinners! This is a long away from "least of the saints" or "least of the apostles," and it is definitely far from the fiery Paul in Galatians who lashes out at his accusers.

What does all this mean? If we long for increase and revival, it will come as we go lower. Understanding who we are *not* makes a big difference. We bear fruit not by thinking more of ourselves and our lives; it comes by knowing that by His grace and mercy alone Christ died and opened up freedom for us forevermore. We must be leaders who want to go lower, not leaders who try to put as many titles on our business cards as possible to somehow compensate for a lack of anointing. We must step into a greater call and go lower.

How low can you go?

In the next chapter we will talk more about how to break barrenness and unbelief. This is a crucial subject. I believe that if we can comprehend this valuable key, mentioned by the apostle Paul, we will be in a position for greatness in the Kingdom.

Let Go

By James Levesque

The mask that you wear can no longer conceal
The truth in your heart and how you feel.
Your heart is starving like a man for a meal,
And you just can't seem to fool people who are real.

You have walked your whole life trying to please others,
And came to church and now please brothers.
You took a look back and walked too far.
You've lived a life, and don't know who you are.

I believe that you will finally get free
When you learn to face current reality.
You hold your feet firm so they won't budge you,
But live in fear that one day they'll judge you.

If they see your struggle, you might be forced
To look at your sin and have a divorce.
Your face can't hide what the soul can see,
And it obvious there's no fruit on this tree.

Believe in yourself, and you might just find
A joyful heart and a beautiful mind.
Assume responsibility; don't live in shame.
Right now all this hiding is hurting His name.

You've embraced your sin like a dog in heat,
And no one else can sit in your seat.
I don't doubt you're gifted and God's given a call.
My concern is all this lying will set up a fall.

Points to Ponder

1. Do you find yourself desiring things like the appearance of gemstones and gold dust more than true revival? If so, what heart motive might be driving this desire?

2. In what areas of your life have you experienced spiritual barrenness?

3. What false finish lines are you celebrating and building monuments to (like Peter on the Mount of Transfiguration) rather than pursuing more of God?

4. In what ways have you tried to reach new levels in the Spirit? Were these things effective, or were they rooted in selfishness?

Chapter 7

BREAKING BARRENNESS PART 2

Love Conquers All

I remember conducting a funeral some years ago. It was my first funeral so I was a bit nervous—never mind the fact that I was only about 24 years old. Death is such a tragic event. Yet it is something all of us will face. The Bible makes it clear that if we are absent from the body, we are present with the Lord (see 2 Cor. 5:8).

Because I was nervous, I sought some counsel and advice about how to do this funeral. I went to the family's house to prepare for the services and talk more about the great man who had died. Although I did not know him personally, I wanted to gain some insight regarding his life. This would help me honor him when I was conducting his memorial service.

I recall walking into this gentleman's family home. I knew he was about 78 years old and had died suddenly. This had come as a bit of a shock to his loved ones. I also had information that he knew the Lord, which was the greatest joy. As I sat there with my pen and pad I was eager to take notes. "Give me some information about Harold," I said. the family had pictures, mementoes, and other artifacts depicting his life; it was beautiful.

Harold had left behind two children and his wife. I inquired about his hobbies, likes, and dislikes, hoping to gather insight into who he really was. The family told me that he loved going to the coffee shop every morning. He would meet the "guys" downtown, have coffee, and shoot the breeze. He also loved crossword puzzles and would sit for hours every day working on them. Knowing he was a believer, I inquired about his church involvement. One of the family members told me he paid tithes and attended services regularly. "He was a member for 25 years," they said. I thought that was beautiful.

I would be lying if I stopped here and told you that was all I found out. I quickly discovered he had lived in fear for a long time. The family broke down and confessed a lot more unhappiness than was initially apparent.

Needless to say, I prayed with this family and made Harold's memorial the best service possible. However, I saw his gravestone awhile back and remember looking at the dash. When most people die, there are two dates on their marker. One is the date they were born, and the other is the date they died; in between is a dash.

What Will You Do With the Dash?

I realized, when I was looking at Harold's gravestone, that life is but a moment. It is a beautiful gift, but it does not last forever, and nothing is guaranteed. I began to think about how hard it was for the family to come up with good things to say about this man, but how easy it was for them to say, "We are just glad he's not suffering on earth anymore."

Please understand that in no way do I devalue a man's life based on works. I do not believe a happy life is works. However, I also do not believe that Jesus died so we can live a life of misery here on earth. We have been given a gift in life. Jesus wants us to have an abundant life, and since that's the case, we can have one. Many of us settle for living beneath the place God has called us to live. We live life by default, not victory.

Today, many of our lives are simply the reaction to a series of bad situations we have experienced. There is little victory. We just respond to one trauma after another. Few are set free. Please hear me out. I have been through hell and back in this life. Those of you who know me and are reading this will surely be nodding your heads in agreement.

I have been in circumstances that some people have never recovered from. (God willing, one day I will write my story.) Each step of the way, I have had to make a decision to live and receive all that God has for me. I am constantly asking myself,

"Is this God's best for me?" because I simply refuse to live anywhere else.

> Many of us settle for living beneath the place God has called us to live. We live life by default, not victory.

I have witnessed two people going through the same trial with two different outlooks and perspectives. Although I understand that everyone is different, devils are all the same. They all torment, steal, rob, and destroy. And they will constantly do that to us if we let them. The only ground the enemy has is the ground we give him.

It amazes me how many people are so focused on the fact that they have not received healing. It's as if God's Word becomes void to them. That's nonsense! I have seen sickness strike my own family, and I have never stopped believing the Word. My mother, as I write this, has multiple sicknesses. Do you think for a moment I will stop praying for the sick? Absolutely not! I will pray for the sick more than ever.

God's Word is greater than our circumstances. There is a vast difference between going through adversity, which we all face at some point, with Christ and His promises and going through it without Him.

We must all decide what we will do with our dash. Whether we like it or not, we are in a fallen world, but Jesus has given us the power to overcome. This is a wonderful day to be alive!

Last night I was in a meeting where we saw a great many miracles. A woman who suffered from a bleeding issue (constant flowing) for 19 years, and who had been told by doctors they could not help her, was completely healed!

Many received salvation, and it was glorious. God healed one lady, who must have been in her 80s, of various diseases, and that was glorious. As she received strength in her body, I began telling her, "The enemy has been telling you to give up and your time is done. I break every lie. I'm telling you that Jesus is going to give you strength, and your work on earth is not finished!"

I watched as she wept and cried. With tears streaming down her face she said, "You mean God can still use me? I'm not too old?" I looked at her, with tears in my eyes, and replied, "No, Mama, God is going to use you mightily." And He will!

It doesn't matter how many years you have felt barren. God wants to fill you with His plan and purpose and give you the greatest life you could ever imagine. Your life is not through. God has not forgotten you. You may feel 100 miles away from God, but He is only one step away!

We must get back to the place of honoring His Word. Honoring His Word will destroy barrenness. Hebrews 11 tells us that faith comes by

> There is a vast difference between going through adversity with Christ and His promises and going through it without Him.

hearing the Word of God. It does not say faith comes from having heard the Word; it is a continual hearing.

Veils

Many people make a lot of claims about Scripture, but they do not believe in their own words. I know many critics who claim to believe the Word of God, yet they do not see the promise of the Word. Paul warned us about this when he wrote:

> We are not like Moses, who would put a veil over his face to prevent the Israelites from gazing at it while the radiance was fading away. But their minds were made dull, for to this day the same veil remains when the old covenant is read. It has not been removed, because only in Christ is it taken away. Even to this day when Moses is read, a veil covers their hearts. But whenever anyone turns to the Lord, the veil is taken away. Now the Lord is the Spirit, and where the Spirit of the Lord is, there is freedom. And we, who with unveiled faces all reflect the Lord's glory, are being transformed into His likeness with ever-increasing glory, which comes from the Lord, who is the Spirit (2 Corinthians 3:13-18 NIV).

Paul's listeners understood the Old Testament, so they understood his reference to the veil. But Paul was saying to them, "Even though through Christ there is no veil, you still read God's Word with a veil over your hearts."

We cannot say we value the Word of God and yet not obey it. The Bible makes a contrast between simply becoming a hearer of the word and being a doer (see James 1:23). We must be doers of the Word. If we value the Bible, then we should live it. Too many people today still live with a veil mindset. The veil is placed over their hearts and minds. Jesus came and ripped the veil forever! We must be empowered to walk in all that God has called us to.

When I became a new believer, someone bought me a Bible. I did not have enough dead service experience to tell me that this book was not powerful. So I picked it up and began to read it. Every day I was blown away by the power of Jesus. I was amazed as I read the stories of God's miracles and healings! I remember going to church believing that God was still going to do what His Word said He did in the past. I could just imagine Him doing these same miracles today. Sometimes I couldn't sleep I was so excited about Jesus moving. Daydreaming about what God could and would do literally kept me up at night.

I Gave Up Drugs for This?

I can remember being in church one Sunday morning feeling so desperate. It was a good service, but I wanted more than good. After church I went to the beach frustrated because I didn't see what I read about in the Bible. I was desperate for mighty deeds! I just knew that Jesus could do more than we could ever imagine.

I knew people left the service that morning sick, depressed, and bound with devils, and I did not feel like that was OK—not if Jesus is alive and well. I walked to the edge of the water, upset with what had not happened at that morning's service. Standing there, I screamed at the top of my lungs, "Is this all I get for the week? Is this it? I gave up sex and drugs for this?"

The thought of giving up my old life to serve a fruitless, empty Christianity was not going to work. I was desperate for much, much more. If we are truly going to read a book that will guide and lead us, then we'd better believe what is in the book.

It was not until I began to put demands on the Word of God that I began to see it for what it really is. God's Word is a great big invitation to a life that we seldom experience. Well, in Jesus' name, that's what we can have!

God's Word is filled with amazing promises. You may not have received any words from the Lord, and you may not have experienced all the dreams and plans in your heart, but it is time for you to sing, "O barren" ones.

Sing, O barren, you who have not borne! Break forth into singing, and cry aloud, you who have not labored with child! For more are the children of the desolate than the children of the married… (Isaiah 54:1).

In this passage, we see a woman who is clearly barren. It is interesting to see what Heaven's remedy for barrenness is; in this Scripture, the Lord tells her to sing! *Sing? Why would He say such a thing?* Singing really does not have a lot to do with being barren. Or does it?

You see, I believe that the greater truth of what is being said is that we need to open our mouths and do something out of faith. Even if we are barren, as we decide to sing, move, and step out in faith and obedience, we will break the curse of barrenness.

I know that God is going to speak to you to move and step out in faith. We will be covering a few keys to increase faith in the next few chapters. I believe that we are about to see a new expression of faith emerge from the last-days Church. It will be glorious!

> It was not until I began to put demands on the Word of God that I began to see it for what it really is.

Love Factor

One of my favorite passages is found in Matthew chapter 10:

> *As you go, preach, saying, "The kingdom of heaven is at hand." Heal the sick, cleanse the lepers, raise the dead, cast out demons. Freely you have received, freely give* (Matthew 10:7-8).

In these verses, Jesus is commissioning the disciples. It is an awesome picture of God sending out His own. Jesus doesn't suggest or ask them to think about it. He commands them to heal the sick, cleanse leapers, and cast out devils.

I know that we are about to see an increase of the resurrection of the dead! We must. Jesus has given us all authority over every demonic power. We are about to see an increase in the expelling of demons. Devils are powerless, and we have all authority! It is interesting that most of us who are sons and daughters of the King do not feel that this is our birthright. It is!

Great Compassion

One day I was praying through these verses and asking God for increase. I felt the Spirit of God say to me, "James, do you want the commissioning of Matthew 10 over your life?" I was not exactly sure what kind of question that was, but either way, the answer was yes. Yes, yes, yes! Then I felt the Lord say, "Then you need to understand why I commissioned them."

> We are about to see an increase of the resurrection of the dead!

As I began to go back and read the verses, I saw a different picture. In Matthew 9, we see what Jesus was doing right before He decided to commission these men.

Then Jesus went about all the cities and villages, teaching in their synagogues, preaching the gospel of the kingdom, and healing every sickness and every disease among the people. But when He saw the multitudes, He was moved with compassion for them, because they were weary and scattered, like sheep having no shepherd. Then He said to His disciples, "The harvest truly is plentiful, but the laborers are few. Therefore pray the Lord of the harvest to send out laborers into His harvest" (Matthew 9:35-38).

It is easy to quote Matthew 10:8 without realizing what Jesus was doing or saying leading up to the commissioning. Jesus did not walk around with an agenda for the day. Many times, on His way to various places and villages, He was led to where the hunger and need was great. Jesus was living the Kingdom, releasing life everywhere He went.

I do not believe that Christ woke up that morning and had it on the agenda to release His disciples. I believe this was in His plan eventually; however, something happened to trigger it on that particular day.

The first thing we notice is that Jesus was going about to all the cities and villages healing every sickness and every disease. This is the mandate of Christ. This is a picture of Jesus doing exactly what He was called to do.

During that time (by the way, it would blow our minds if we knew all the details as He was healing every sickness and every disease!), He *stopped*. What in the world would cause Jesus to pause from healing every sickness? The Bible says it was compassion. Jesus had such compassion for people.

That Scripture alone exposes a great key to seeing the touch of God move through our lives, thus breaking barren areas: we need compassion. We must have a genuine love for people. Too many ministers today are

> Jesus always has and always will touch the ones who are close to Him.

angry with people. Miracles and healings will not flow from an angry minister—not for any length of time, that's for sure.

Love has to be our core motivation for everything. It is out of a love for people that we give ourselves as servants to a lost and dying world. Compassion, just like Jesus had, must be what causes us to lament for the poor, the sick, and the broken.

Here is Jesus, walking and demonstrating the Kingdom, and then he stops as compassion comes over Him. He begins to turn to the ones closest to Him. That is no different today; Jesus always has and always will touch the ones who are close to Him. He looks at His disciples and He tells them that the harvest is plentiful and the laborers are few. Again, this does not mean that He is only calling a few; it means that only a few are answering the call! The situation is no different today.

Jesus is sharing His compassion and concern for all these lost people. Then out of compassion and love, He releases His disciples and commissions them. Did you catch that? Jesus gave them all power and authority. He commissioned after *compassion* and *love* built the need.

Power With a Purpose

What is your motivation for ministry? What is your core motivation for seeing the anointing move in and through your life? If it is not love, it will not last. Love must be the anchor for all things. The power of God must always be connected to the purpose of God. We need God's power to touch a lost and hurting world. The world needs to know that Jesus Christ saves, delivers, and heals. As you and I receive the love of God and compassion for others, we have set the foundation for true power to flow.

> The true power of God will flow out of a deep desire to see others set free!

We must continue to look through the eyes of love. Too many evangelists today are angry men and women. They are constantly telling hurting people how hurt they are. That makes no sense to me. It is rubbish to think that Christ would walk around the earth today sharing anything but good news. Many self-proclaimed "soul winners" are walking around with no power. They have some demonic anointing of anger and think that will be enough. I believe that when they get delivered of devils, then they can set others free.

Jesus always released power with compassion. I invite you into a life of love and compassion. The true power of God will flow out of a deep desire to see others set free! Get burdened for the lost!

What Will You Do With Your Dash?

By James Levesque

Life is but an instance; it may come and go.
You're privileged to live, so you should also know
That at the end of your life it's not houses or cash,
Just merely, what have you done with your dash?

Your dash is something that you can't take back.
It's more than a result of a fatal heart attack,
More than a bunch of U.S. bonds you can save.
*I'm talking about **the dash** between the dates on your grave.*

When all is said and done and the grave is intact,
The question will be, did you make an impact?
Regardless of the answer, you can't rewind,
If the truth is you died and left nothing behind…

It's like starting a race, beginning at the pole.
You can gain the whole world, yet lose your soul.
That's not a way to live and ultimately wrong
If you start out great, but don't finish strong.

Drama doesn't matter, and forget about strife.
I refuse to live like I wasted a life.
Through this poem, I'll be the first to give
The fact in life, you have a purpose to live.

I've said for sure, life will get the best of me.
At that point, you will find your destiny.
Choose a life of meaning; your heart will surely melt,
So, long after you go, your life will be felt.

Points to Ponder

1. Is the life you're living God's best for you? If not, what is? What can you do to point yourself in that direction?

2. What will you do with your dash? What is the inner resolve of your heart?

3. Are there ways in which you read the Bible with a veil over your heart? When you read the Bible, do you purpose to obey everything you read, or do you often find yourself making excuses?

4. Have you ever "put a demand" on the promises of the Word of God? What happened? In what areas of your life do you need to step into faith and believe God for overcoming power?

Chapter 8

REVELATION

Jesus Christ Unveiled

The word *revelation* means to lift the veil. We all need more of it. However, revelation has received a weird vibe because of flakey people who do not understand it. If we are truly going to experience an increase of God's presence and power in our lives, we must receive revelation.

In no way do I mean going beyond the Bible or becoming extra-biblical. God has given us His Holy Spirit without measure. He will never contradict His Word. He will, however, contradict your opinion of His Word.

Consider the great evangelists and revivalists of yesterday. Men like George Whitfield. Gilbert Tennant, Jonathan Edwards, and John Wesley were among those whom God used to bring an awakening—a God-consciousness—to society. When these men preached, they spoke of a "new conversion experience" in the light of being born again. When they preached and the Word of God went forth, many people prayed and fasted for days, and sometimes weeks, until they experienced a sense of "release." Only then did they feel like they were truly saved.

This is a far cry from today. We know and understand that whosoever calls upon the name of the Lord shall be saved. Period! We understand that salvation comes through grace—the grace bestowed on us when Jesus died on the cross and paid the price for it. We do not have to pay for it again.

But these believers were not wrong. They simply were operating under the revelation they had at that time. Now we can see how that revelation has grown. The same can be said about divine healing. In the early days, people believed that through faith they could see people healed in their bodies. But many also believed that God put sickness on people. They had an Old Testament understanding of God's nature. We understand today that sickness comes from sin and as the result of many roots. But either way, God's mercy and love will always desire to heal.

> If we are truly going to experience an increase of God's presence and power in our lives, we must receive revelation.

Whether healing takes place or not, the nature of God is never negated.

Today we can see how revelation has grown in various ways. The early church believed that tongues were the initial and only evidence of the infilling of the Holy Ghost. Now, we clearly see that is not the case. Tongues are one evidence, but not the only evidence, of being filled with the Spirit. Jesus did not say, "You will receive tongues after the Holy Ghost comes upon you." That's just foolish. He said, "You will receive power..." (see Acts 1:8).

Jesus continued, "...and you shall be My witnesses..." The reason we receive power is to be a witness! The indwelling of the Holy Ghost is evidenced by boldness, power, presence, and many other factors.

Revelation of Jesus Christ

So *revelation* is often misunderstood. Scripture tells us:

That the genuineness of your faith, being much more precious than gold that perishes, though it is tested by fire, may be found to praise, honor, and glory at the revelation of Jesus Christ (1 Peter 1:7).

Here is the key to revelation: it is Jesus Christ! If we desire revelation, then we need to understand that it will be the revelation of Jesus. We cannot seek or get revelation any other way; it is of Jesus Christ.

Many people think revelation is "goose bumps" or even a hyped service. They are sadly mistaken. Trust me, not many people are actually receiving biblical revelation. Many are just people who chase feelings. They feed off an earthly lust of attention, and their lives seldom produce fruit. Everyone with an ounce of truth can see and discern this.

It is these folks who hurt and set back the Body of Christ. As long as we continue to tolerate shallow believers who have never been changed by the power of God, we are in trouble. We need more. We

Here is the key to revelation: it is Jesus Christ!

need revelation. But it must be of Jesus Christ. If we think that we have seen and understand all of who Jesus is, we are deceived. This gift of life we have been given in Christ is an invitation to more.

Sozo

What if I gave you a car, a Ferrari? Let's say I walked into your house and gave it to you as a gift. I just handed you the keys and told you that it was right outside. Then you picked up the phone and told everyone you knew that you had received this gift. That would be awesome. However, if I revisited your home a few weeks later only to find out that you had never walked out of the house and gotten in your car, that would be a problem.

Furthermore, imagine I stopped by a few years later only to discover that you indeed went outside, opened the door, and drove the car—but only around your parking lot. Even if you were satisfied and content, at the end of the day, you had still never really operated the car. If I gave you a Ferrari and after years and years you had only managed to drive it a few feet, that would be frustrating. Here I gave you a fast car, and you have never experienced what it can do!

Of course, our Father in Heaven is no earthly man, and He does not get frustrated. However, we have been given a gift from God that we have not yet fully opened. For years we have been taught how to operate something that few people fully operate.

In First Peter 1:3-5, we find another powerful Scripture regarding this.

> *Praise be to the God and Father of our Lord Jesus Christ!*
> *In His great mercy He has given us new birth into a living*
> *hope through the resurrection of Jesus Christ from the*
> *dead, and into an inheritance that can never perish, spoil*
> *or fade—kept in heaven for you, who through faith are*
> *shielded by God's power until the coming of the salvation*
> *that is ready to be revealed in the last time* (NIV).

There is a "ready to be revealed" salvation awaiting us! Of course, we are saved. Of course, we are born again. But there is more the Father wants to show us. We have not fully seen what the true expression of this gift is.

It's not that God is hiding it away. It is that we have not understood the gift and are blind. There is such a great salvation we still need to experience. Jesus did not die on the cross so that we can go to church. Jesus did not die so that we can live a partial life of victory and blessing. We need to experience all that God has for us.

Hosea 4:6 says, *"My people are destroyed for lack of knowledge…."* We need to understand why a lack of knowledge, or vision, can and will cause us to perish. How can someone be destroyed simply by living an unfruitful and barren life here on earth? Many people today have become comfortable living below the level of awareness God has called them to. If we come to Christianity and simply play a part-time role, never experiencing victory, we have just traded one form of bondage for another.

I remember Leonard Ravenhill saying, "The church today wants to be raptured from the role of responsibility." Because of a lack of freedom and victory, we get into a mindset that desires escape. We think a victorious life is not for us. But the greatest years of our lives are ahead of us! We will finish and do all that God has for us to do. We simply need vision! We need revelation! That's what will enable us to finish strong.

One may ask, "Why do we need revelation when the doctrines have been established and set?" Revelation is not creating doctrine; revelation is allowing us to live the doctrine we believe.

Getting Out of the Natural

We see an example of this in the Book of John. John 4 tells us that Jesus met a woman at Jacob's well. When He walked up to the woman by the well, He graced her and made the most powerful statement: *"Give Me a drink"* (John 4:7).

> Revelation is not creating doctrine; revelation is allowing us to live the doctrine we believe.

The woman replied: *"How is it that You, being a Jew, ask a drink from me, a Samaritan woman?"* (John 4:9). In the time of Jesus, Jews had no dealings with Samaritans.

This is the first opportunity this woman missed. Here was Jesus, the most powerful man—God in the flesh—who has ever lived. He speaks a few words, and people are healed, delivered, and raised from the dead. He asked this lady for a drink, though He clearly was not thirsty. He was giving her an opportunity to receive freedom and to understand who she truly was. Jesus was initiating the opportunity of a lifetime. The multitudes flocked to Him, but here He was coming to her.

Obviously, this is her first chance to understand, and she didn't get it. She reverted to the natural. Then Jesus said: *"If you knew the gift of God, and who it is who says to you, 'Give Me a drink,' you would have asked Him, and He would have given you living water"* (John 4:10).

So Jesus, in His love and mercy, told her, essentially, "I am not here for a natural encounter; I am here for a deeper cause." And she responded: *"Sir, You have nothing to draw with, and the well is deep. Where then do You get that living water?"* (John 4:11).

Here is the second missed opportunity for freedom. Jesus was not talking about water. There is no Jesus beverage called "living water." At that moment, she really believed that He was offering her a beverage! So Jesus, in His love and mercy, kept going—trying to give her a chance for freedom.

> Whoever drinks of this water will thirst again, but whoever drinks of the water that I shall give him will never thirst. But the water I shall give him will become in him a fountain of water springing up into everlasting life (John 4:13-14).

Jesus made it clear as day that He was not there for natural reasons. He even went as far as saying that this natural water would not satisfy and that what He had to give would eternally satisfy. He also mentioned that something would happen on the inside of her. He could not have been more clear!

Let's see what she thought: "Sir, give me this water, that I may not thirst, nor come here to draw" (John 4:15). Here is the third missed opportunity. Jesus was not talking about the natural. But she kept on bringing up the natural.

In the same way, we cannot continue to approach a supernatural God naturally. We will miss what the Lord is trying to tell us.

Thank God that Jesus was loving and patient and saw her heart and decided to keep speaking to her. In John 4:16, He said: "Go, call your husband, and come here." Jesus decided to speak into her past, revealing secrets no one knew.

Her response: *"I have no husband"* (John 4:17). Here is the fourth missed opportunity. Jesus did not speak in the natural to her at any time during their conversation. But she kept speaking in the flesh. Scripture is filled with nonbelievers who heard one word from Christ and were changed, and this woman missed four opportunities for her life to be changed.

Christ now made it personal. He decided to touch on an area few knew about. After she said she didn't have a husband, Christ began to prophetically open up her heart by revealing five husbands in her past and a current messed up relationship. After practically hearing Jesus bring her whole past life before her, she missed yet another opportunity. This was the fifth time He tried, and she said, *"Sir, I perceive that You are a prophet. Our fathers, worshipped on this mountain and you Jews say in Jerusalem is the place where one ought to worship"* (John 4:19-20).

This is a valuable lesson regarding how revelation operates. Many times Christ will try to speak truth that would set us free. But we are stuck on what we have always known and cannot or chose not to hear. Our measuring stick for the future cannot be the lack we have seen in the past. In this hour, Jesus is speaking more clearly than He ever has, and many of us continue to revert to that which we have always known.

The danger in such a pattern is that when Christ comes to give us revelation, truth that will add to what we are operating in, we cannot continue to operate under what we already know. The Bible is a guidebook for living a meaningful life—a life of power and love. We cannot continue to say we believe in the Word of God yet not live it out.

Jesus must alter our human-made doctrines and theologies so that we can live His Word. Many of us have been stuck in institutionalized Christianity and have had our ability to understand truth stolen from us. Jesus Himself said He was the way, the truth, and the life (see John 14:6). Yet we continue to settle for people's regurgitated doctrine of devils, while Jesus is offering a better way.

> Our measuring stick for the future cannot be the lack we have seen in the past.

I remember when I was first born again and saw folks praying for the sick. People would say, "If it's your will, Lord, heal them," or "God, I ask that You would heal so and so." As I began to read my Bible, I realized that I could not find any Scriptures to back up those types of prayers. I looked at the accounts of Jesus' ministry, and it was completely different. When Jesus healed the sick, He cursed sickness and commanded life (see Matt. 8:8,13,16; Mark 1:23-26; 7:32-35; Luke 7:14; 9:42; 13:11-13).

This is difficult for many believers today because they do not operate in biblical authority. But when I began to adjust my prayers, results began to happen. I would no longer beg devils or God. I would simply do what Jesus did—command life in His name! I came to realize that many of our spiritual patterns have come from men and women who were barren or operating in a truth that had not been fulfilled.

The Word of God is our final authority. If we do not see a biblical pattern at least three times throughout Scripture, then we have no business creating a doctrine out of something.

In the Book of Galatians, we see Paul addressing a few churches regarding false doctrinal issues. The elders in some of these churches were rising up and saying Paul's Gospel message was not valid. Paul began to address some of these issues in the first few chapters, where we find him saying:

> But I make known to you, brethren, that the Gospel which was preached by me is not according to man. For I neither received it by man, nor was I taught it, but it came through the revelation of Jesus Christ (Galatians 1:11-12).

Paul addressed this concern by saying his message did not come by people; it came by a revelation of Jesus Christ.

We need a revelation of Jesus Christ. It is not what is in His hands; it is Him. I do not look at Jesus Christ as separate from miracles and power. The source is all the same. When we receive Christ, everything that Christ is and represents is in us. We must continue to seek the truth that will set us free. If we really find value in the Bible, then we must be willing to learn who Jesus is and learn His ways. It's time that the veil over our heads and hearts is removed!

I believe that you will walk in the fullness of Jesus as He reveals more of His nature to you.

Points to Ponder

1. Have you ever realized that something you believed about the Bible or God was wrong? What did you learn from having God challenge your opinion of His Word?

2. Honestly evaluating your life using the analogy of the Ferrari, have you learned to drive the car to its fullest potential, or are you just taking it around the parking lot? Why?

3. Explain how revelation enables you to live the doctrine you believe. In what areas do you need greater revelation of Jesus?

4. In what ways are you interpreting the Bible and your future based on your past experiences rather than on what the Bible literally says? Ask the Lord to give you a revelation of His truth in these areas.

Chapter 9

FAITH FACTOR

The Faith That Increases

I am blessed to live in the New England region of America. Not too long ago, I was at a conference with a well-known minister. He was telling me about his passion to know about revival history and how he had acquired some of the most rare revival artifacts that were around.

As I was driving back to the hotel, I realized that one of my desires is to have a collection of revival artifacts. I said, "Lord, I want a collection of revival history." I quickly heard, "I've given it to you in the land of New England." When the Lord told me that, I knew exactly what He was saying.

New England is a place that has witnessed God move in the past. This land has seen the paths of John Wesley, George Whitfield, and Frank Sandford. No one interested in revival could forget the powerful events that took place in Enfield, Connecticut. Jonathan Edwards came to a tiny little church and spoke a message entitled "Sinners in the Hands of an Angry God," and it sparked the First Great Awakening around the world!

> Faith demands and commands; merely hoping only suggests.

I was born and raised in Groton, Connecticut, and as I began to research revival history, I realized how many times God's power was revealed in this beautiful land.

Not too long ago, my wife and I took close ministry friends, Jerame and Miranda Nelson, to see the First Great Awakening site in Enfield. It was a cold, snowy afternoon, and we were driving around searching for the site. Finally my wife remembered the general area where the memorial was located. When we stumbled upon the rock that marks the site, we began to pray and cry out for another great awakening in America.

As we were praying, the Lord began to speak to me. "I am releasing a gift of faith in this hour to those who will believe for a massive harvest of souls," He said. I realized in that moment that God's desire is that we would walk and operate in a great realm of faith!

The Bible speaks of a deposit of faith that we all have (see Luke 17:6). There is also a gift of faith (see 1 Cor 12:7-9). When we talk about faith, people have many different views. In the Book of Hebrews, the Bible tells us: *"Now faith is the substance of things hoped for, the evidence of things not seen"* (Heb. 11:1).

Evidence and *substance* are tangible words. The very nature of faith is a guarantee. Many people confuse faith with hope and, as a result, many believers end up disappointed, with their lives bearing little fruit. Faith demands and commands; merely hoping only suggests.

Faith Opens Eyes

Faithless Christianity produces blind followers. Partial faith will not get us very far in this hour. Jesus desires for us to walk in the same power and might that He walked in! In Second Kings chapter 6 we see a great example of this: "*...Then the Lord opened the servant's eyes, and he looked and saw the hills full of horses and chariots of fire all around Elisha*" (2 Kings 6:17 NIV).

Gehazi and Elisha are together in the midst of battle, and Gehazi looks out the window and sees that armies are coming to attack from everywhere. He quickly notices that they are greatly outnumbered. Like most folks, he says,

God is going to rip every scale from our eyes and show us that we have the victory!

"What are we going to do?" They were clearly not the majority, so how could Elisha's response make any sense? "*Those who are with us are more than those who are with them*" (2 Kings 6:16). No, they are not! Not in the natural sense. Anyone with two eyes could see that they were surely outnumbered. But then

Elisha prayed for Gehazi that his eyes would be opened. And God opened his eyes.

What happened when God opened Gehazi's eyes? He began to see in another dimension! He began to see with the eyes of the Spirit. Just a second before, he had looked and only saw in a natural ability; suddenly he could see in the Spirit, and he saw a dimension of the Kingdom he could not see otherwise.

Many of us are just like Gehazi. We have become so accustomed to looking through our natural lenses that the reality of the supernatural is quenched. We fight battles and go through life with a defensive, cautious approach. We may even feel like we are defeated most of the time. But God is going to rip every scale from our eyes and show us that we have the victory! This Scripture is a great example to us. Faith allows us to stand in the midst of every circumstance and see God's point of view.

Birthing Promises

Faith empowers and enables us to birth the very promises and destiny God has for us. I have travelled to various places where people have become so used to hearing prophecy that they are almost immune to it. I have gone to churches where I have spoken accurate prophetic words in the past, and people will hint and almost try to manipulate because they want to hear from God.

In one such church, I was praying and asking the Lord if He had a specific directional word He wanted me to release over this place, and to my sudden amazement, I heard, *"No!"* Let me note, I am not talking about salvation and miracles. Healings and the demonstration of God are always present and will happen anywhere that Jesus is. What God has spoken to me is that He indeed has directional words to release over many regions.

However, because many people do not heed or respond to the words they receive, they are hindered from moving forward.

> Expectation is what
> releases faith.

I believe that the greatest demonstrations and words have yet to be released. I also believe that if we, as a corporate Body, are faithful to what God is speaking, a greater measure will be released for us to walk in. As we are faithful with little, God will allow us to be faithful with much.

Jesus, in the Book of Acts, gave a group of believers a great instruction: *"…He gave them this command: 'Do not leave Jerusalem, but wait for the gift My Father promised, which you have heard Me speak about'"* (Acts 1:4 NIV).

I want to make a few clear observations here. For starters, Jesus did *not* say, "You shall receive tongues after the Holy Spirit comes upon you." As we saw earlier, He said they would receive power. Also, He asked them to tarry until they received the gift.

So here are many believers waiting and contending for ten days, not fully understanding or knowing what was about to happen. Imagine waiting in the upper room and all you knew was Jesus said you would receive a greater measure of power! Today some people cannot contend for ten minutes, never mind ten days.

It's not about a timeframe; it's an expectation. Expectation is what releases faith. If you have ever been around someone who is a faith-filled believer and is always expectant, it is contagious. The same desire that caused those mighty saints to tarry is birthed in us! We must walk in a realm of expectation and faith. This is the great key of faith—always expecting God to move wherever we go.

Get Ready for a Harvest!

While I was in prayer a few months back, the Lord really impressed on me that I was about to walk and live in a greater dimension of faith. Shortly after that, I was ministering at a large conference in Canada where I was preaching about the blessing of the Lord and sharing how we have been freed from the curse.

At the end of the meeting, I knew that God wanted to break out in a great measure. I told the people, "I want everyone who has devils to come to my left for prayer, and if you are here for healing in your body, come to my right for prayer." I was shocked as over 800 people ran forward! I quickly grabbed a few ministers to help pray.

We were there for hours praying for those filled with demons and those who were sick. I watched in excitement as Jesus began to set people free and heal their bodies. A few of the most notable ones were a girl with a broken ankle, many people with devils (with manifestations), and a young man with cerebral palsy who jumped off the floor and began to walk and run for the first time.

It was glorious! After I left the meeting, many people were stunned at the number of testimonies and manifestations. People even came up to me and said, "You should leave New England and pack out stadiums" and, "Let's do extended meetings and call this revival!" I left the area fast and went to Wendy's to eat a burger with some friends.

Later that night, the Lord spoke to me and said, "Don't fall for any man-made ideas. I want to do this in every meeting!" Three weeks later, I received an e-mail from that church. They listed over 100 confirmed miracles and deliverances from that night. Although it may seem small, I know that God is stretching our understanding for increase!

I was in Vermont the following week, and again I witnessed a great display of God's power. I was preaching at an awesome place that I have been to before, a place where it is normal for people to bring drug addicts and others to be set free.

This time was different. When I arrived at the church (we were outside in a tent), I was met in the parking lot by a very drunk lady. She began to curse at me and yell as my wife and I walked in. I was kind of shocked and thought she must be crazy to talk to me like that. I began to minister and speak a word I had for the ministry, and as I spoke, the drunk woman stood up and cursed at me in the meeting! I have not had that happen before; when someone attempted disruption in a meeting, I had just shut the foolishness down. But after I repeatedly told her to stop, she just got louder and angrier.

> *Every* person who needed a healing was healed!

As I preached, it was evident that people were distracted. So without any feelings, any goose bumps, or anything, I said, "OK, that's it. I want every sick person here to come to the front, and I believe God wants to move here today!" Immediately people began to come up front for healing. Of course, Miss Drunk Lady was right there watching. As I began to pray, Jesus was healing bodies—creative miracles and all!

And a major breakthrough occurred. *Every* person who needed a healing was healed! Many there had never witnessed that before—*every person!* Come on, Doctor Jesus! Also, after the last person was prayed for, I began to prophecy over a few people the Lord led me to. Just when I finished, and it was clear God had shown up in power, the drunken woman ran up to me yelling. She pushed me, and as she did, she yelled, "What about me?" She saw God break through in everyone's life and realized her own need for a breakthrough.

At that moment, God started speaking through me. She already knew that God was moving and was touched herself. God rocked her life with demonstration! It spoke so much to me that night. I knew that the fact that every person said they were healed spoke of a greater opportunity to believe for. Imagine that everywhere we go, the Spirit is willing and ready to heal all!

Your Tongue: Faith's Tool

A secret to faith is found in Proverbs 18:21, *"Death and life are in the power of tongue...."*

I remember reading this Scripture as a new believer and being astonished. I looked around at all the people who were struggling spiritually, and then I began to look at people who walked in a great dimension of faith, and I realized that men and women of great faith know and exercise this tool—the tongue!

As ugly as it may be—fat or skinny, bad breath and all—the tongue carries the very power of life and death. The power of words is real. I understand that others have taken this concept and exaggerated and manipulated it, but that does not weaken the truth at hand.

As we read the Scriptures, we see a power released through words. Consider Jesus. He did not walk the earth and beg for healing and deliverance. He simply commanded it. His words were a reflection of His heart and devotion.

Some words have no power, while others do. The difference is the *heart* behind the words. We may speak life, or we may speak death, but chances are, we are going to speak. Second Corinthians 4:13 presents this concept: "...*We also believe and therefore speak.*"

We are called to speak what we believe. As followers of Jesus Christ, we are to walk in faith, and a great measure of our faith is what we speak. Here's a thought: If we are called to speak what we believe, then if we don't speak, does that mean we don't believe?

As ugly as it may be the tongue carries the very power of life and death.

Have you ever met someone who is very negative? They seem to speak everything this earth or the enemy speaks to them. They are like a parrot for the enemy! "I will never be used by God." "I don't have any gifts." "We are so poor." "We are always broke." You know the people I mean.

But Paul the apostle gave us a different set of instructions when he wrote:

...*Whatever is true, whatever is noble, whatever is right, whatever is pure, whatever is lovely, whatever is admirable—if anything is excellent or praiseworthy— think about such things* (Philippians 4:8 NIV).

Why would Paul instruct us to think about these things? I believe one reason is because sometimes, in life, there are circumstances that do not seem great in the natural. As believers, we must be able to look past the negative and find something worth praising God for. Negative Nancy will rarely see breakthrough. We must decree life over every situation and circumstance. That does not mean turning a blind eye to the undesirable, but rather keeping life on our lips and finding something to give thanks for!

Giving Thanks

I am reminded of the time Jesus had over 5,000 people to feed. The disciples were a bit worried, and in the natural, they did not see a way to feed

> When we give thanks for a little, we will see a lot.

all of these people with a boy's lunch. To be honest, that boy's lunch would not have fed me! Looking to Jesus, the disciples could not have guessed what would come out of our Lord's mouth. Would He command them to feed everyone? Would He tell them they had no faith? What would Jesus do? Well, here is what He did: *"Then He took the seven loaves and the fish, and when had had given thanks..."* (Matt. 15:36 NIV).

What? Are you kidding me? Did Jesus just take that lunch and give thanks? I am sure no one saw that coming. But just after He gave thanks, they fed everyone and had 12 baskets left over! *Wow!* I believe that, in Jesus' demonstration, we witnessed a powerful tool: *Give thanks!* No matter what, where, who, how, or why, we must give thanks. When we give thanks for a little, we will see a lot. Jesus is our example!

Are you ready to see multiplication? Give thanks. Do you long to see increase in every area of your life? Give thanks. There are times when I will stop everything and find something to give thanks for. The power of life is in your tongue.

The tongue has the power to sink or guide a ship. We love to hear about life coming from our tongues; however, death can also come. We can hinder God's work with our tongues of unbelief. Jesus said:

> But I say to you that for every idle word men speak, they will give account of it in the day of judgment. For by your words you will be justified, and by your words you will be condemned (Matthew 12:36-37).

Yes, we will be judged for every idle word. We will be justified or condemned by our words. I believe this is a judgment, but I also I believe that we have condemned ourselves to some degree. We will be the prophets of our own lives. We must believe God's report over the report of the enemy.

Even though there are tangible earthly circumstances that may be against you, I exhort you to go to the Word of God. Find every promise and decree it over your life! Jesus is always greater. Remember: "*...He who is in you is greater than he who is in the* *world*" (1 John 4:4). This does not say, "He who is *with* you." No! It says, "He who is *in* you"!

Preach, Proclaim, and Declare

In Isaiah 61:1-2, we find a familiar passage of Scripture.

The Spirit of the Lord God is upon Me, because the Lord has anointed Me to preach good tidings to the poor; He has sent me to heal the brokenhearted, to proclaim liberty to the captives, and the opening of the prison to those who are bound; to proclaim the acceptable year of the Lord, and the day of vengeance of our God....

What an inheritance! The Spirit of the Lord is upon me because He has anointed me. Amen! We are anointed. Don't ever forget that. The reason for that anointing is to preach the Gospel, set captives free, and proclaim God's favor!

As we read that passage, it is interesting to note that every anointed action we are called to do is through speaking. Can we really set captives free with our words? Can we proclaim God's freedom and favor with words and see it manifest? The answer is yes. More than yes, we are anointed by God to do it! We are empowered to speak and set captives free. We are already empowered to preach God's Word. Now we have to believe it.

In Isaiah 42:20-22, we see a group of people who are bound. They need freedom and have not been delivered:

"Seeing many things, but you do not observe; opening the ears, but he does not hear." The Lord is well pleased for His righteousness' sake; He will exalt the law and make it honorable. But this is a people robbed and plundered; all of them are snared in holes, and they are hidden in prison houses; they are for prey, and no one delivers; for plunder, and no one says, "Restore!"

These people are "snared in holes." They are prey and no one delivers; they are plundered and no one says restore. Again we see that true deliverance and freedom are needed and that a faith-filled tongue will set them free!

Where do you need deliverance? What mountain is in front of you? It's time to wield your spiritual weapon. It's in

> Every anointed action we are called to do is through speaking.

your mouth. As you begin to speak and declare life, the very kingdom of darkness will flee. That's a promise! So begin to declare life, and I will agree with you also for freedom. Say this prayer along with me and believe for the victory!

*Father, I thank You, in Jesus' name, for the power and anointing to declare freedom. In Jesus' name, I take authority over every mindset that is not from You. Father, I thank You now for freedom—freedom over my finances, marriage, ministry, job, and mind! Lord, I declare life and freedom over every area **now**!*

And I thank You for increase and favor. Holy Spirit, I submit every area of my life to You and give You full control to speak to me and help me speak life every day! In Jesus' name, amen.

This will be a great new season for you. Let this be more than a prayer. Let it be a lifestyle in the Kingdom of God. Remember to give thanks in every situation! I am excited about the new victories ahead!

Changing of the Guard

By James Levesque

Eli has fallen and died in his chair,
and fear-based religion will die if you dare!
The hand of tyranny that once ruled our lives
is destroyed and demolished for freedom in Christ.

Control and anger from Eli will heed
to a new generation; it's Samuel's breed.
We've heard the Lord's voice and heeded His call.
The priest said, "Lie down! It was nothing at all."

Confidence now reigns; the Lord can be heard.
Eli is slumped over—not even a word!
As I remember the years that Eli led,
the Spirit was quenched and his words just seemed dead.

He would rather see law resurrect over life,
but the priesthood is filled with anger and strife.
My heart is not bitter; at times it travails.
I've learned now what happens when fathering fails...

That strong iron fist won't raise up a son.
What child can succeed when his dad has a gun?
And it's not what you think; it's a spiritual one
to kill all our dreams and make sure that they're done.

God's not calling us where everyone goes,
just where absolute love and fathering flows...
Our cry is that fathers would return to their heart,
and loving their children would begin from the start.

The Spirit of Eli has died in this land
so that Samuel may come and grab the Lord's hand.

Points to Ponder

1. What is the difference between faith and hope? In what areas of your life are you living in hope rather than faith?

2. Do you most often see the circumstances of life according to your natural eyes or the eyes of the Spirit? How does that affect your stance in life?

3. Are you a person of expectation—always expecting God to move wherever you go? How can you cultivate greater expectation in your heart?

4. Is your speech primarily negative or primarily positive? What can you do to help yourself respond with life-filled and thankful words in any circumstance?

ABOUT JAMES LEVESQUE

James Levesque serves as an international speaker, a church planter, and a young, emerging apostolic voice in New England and across America. His heart is to see awakening and revival overtake Christianity and every culture. Currently, James, along with his wife Debbie, pastor and lead Engaging Heaven Center, a church located in New London, Connecticut. It exists to establish a culture of revival through radical obedience.

Visit James' Website at:

www.engagingheaven.com

IN THE RIGHT HANDS, THIS BOOK WILL CHANGE LIVES!

Most of the people who need this message will not be looking for this book. To change their lives, you need to put a copy of this book in their hands.

> *But others (seeds) fell into good ground, and brought forth fruit, some a hundred-fold, some sixty-fold, some thirty-fold* (Matthew 13:8).

Our ministry is constantly seeking methods to find the good ground, the people who need this anointed message to change their lives. Will you help us reach these people?

> *Remember this—a farmer who plants only a few seeds will get a small crop. But the one who plants generously will get a generous crop* (2 Corinthians 9:6).

EXTEND THIS MINISTRY BY SOWING
3 BOOKS, 5 BOOKS, 10 BOOKS, **OR MORE TODAY,**
AND BECOME A LIFE CHANGER!

Thank you,

Don Nori Sr., Founder
Destiny Image
Since 1982

DESTINY IMAGE PUBLISHERS, INC.

*"Speaking to the Purposes of God for This Generation
and for the Generations to Come."*

VISIT OUR NEW SITE HOME AT
WWW.DESTINYIMAGE.COM

FREE SUBSCRIPTION TO DI NEWSLETTER

Receive free unpublished articles by top DI authors, exclusive

discounts, and free downloads from our best and newest books.

Visit www.destinyimage.com to subscribe.

Write to: Destiny Image
              P.O. Box 310
              Shippensburg, PA 17257-0310

Call: 1-800-722-6774

Email: orders@destinyimage.com

For a complete list of our titles or to place an order
online, visit www.destinyimage.com.